THE
BIBLE
PROMISE
BOOK

D1007572

BARBOUR
PUBLISHING

ESPECIALLY FOR

FROM

DATE

© 2013 by Barbour Publishing, Inc.

Print ISBNs
978-1-62029-750-6
978-1-62029-751-3
978-1-62029-752-0
978-1-62029-753-7

eBook Editions:
Adobe Digital Edition (.epub)
978-1-62029-983-8
Kindle and MobiPocket Edition (.prc)
978-1-62029-982-1

All scripture quotations are taken from the King James Version of the Bible.

Published by Barbour Publishing, Inc., P.O. Box 719, Uhrichsville, Ohio 44683, www.barbourbooks.com

Our mission is to publish and distribute inspirational products offering exceptional value and biblical encouragement to the masses.

Member of the
Evangelical Christian
Publishers Association

Printed in China.

CONTENTS

INTRODUCTION

Whatever the need of the moment, the answer is to be found in scripture, if we take the time to search for it. Whatever we're feeling, whatever we're suffering, whatever we're hoping, the Bible has something to say to us.

This collection of Bible verses is meant for use as a handy reference when you need the Bible's guidance on a particular problem in your life. It is in no way intended to replace regular Bible study or the use of a concordance for in-depth study of a subject. There are many facets of your life and many topics in the Bible that are not covered here.

But if, for example, you are feeling extremely lonely one day, some of the Bible's wisdom and comfort is available to you here under the topic of *Loneliness*. All topics are arranged alphabetically, for ease of use.

All scripture is from the King James Version of the Bible.

ANGER

The LORD is gracious, and full
of compassion; slow to anger,
and of great mercy.
PSALM 145:8

> A God ready to pardon, gracious
> and merciful, slow to anger,
> and of great kindness. . .
> NEHEMIAH 9:17

For his anger endureth but a moment;
in his favour is life: weeping may
endure for a night, but joy cometh
in the morning.
PSALM 30:5

> Wherefore, my beloved brethren,
> let every man be swift to hear,
> slow to speak, slow to wrath:
> For the wrath of man worketh
> not the righteousness of God.
> JAMES 1:19–20

Be not hasty in thy spirit to be angry:
for anger resteth in the bosom of fools.
ECCLESIASTES 7:9

> He that is slow to anger is better
> than the mighty; and he that ruleth
> his spirit than he that taketh a city.
> PROVERBS 16:32

He that is soon angry dealeth foolishly.
PROVERBS 14:17

A wrathful man stirreth up strife: but he
that is slow to anger appeaseth strife.
PROVERBS 15:18

An angry man stirreth up strife,
and a furious man aboundeth in
transgression.
PROVERBS 29:22

Cease from anger, and forsake wrath:
fret not thyself in any wise to do evil.
PSALM 37:8

Make no friendship with an angry
man; and with a furious man thou
shalt not go: Lest thou learn his ways,
and get a snare to thy soul.
PROVERBS 22:24–25

A soft answer turneth away wrath:
but grievous words stir up anger.
PROVERBS 15:1

Fathers, provoke not your children
to anger, lest they be discouraged.
COLOSSIANS 3:21

Be ye angry, and sin not: let not
the sun go down upon your wrath.
EPHESIANS 4:26

The discretion of a man deferreth
his anger; and it is his glory to
pass over a transgression.
PROVERBS 19:11

It is better to dwell in the wilderness,
than with a contentious and
an angry woman.
PROVERBS 21:19

But I say unto you, That whosoever is
angry with his brother without a cause
shall be in danger of the judgment.
MATTHEW 5:22

Let all bitterness, and wrath, and anger,
and clamour, and evil speaking, be put
away from you, with all malice: And be
ye kind one to another, tenderhearted,
forgiving one another, even as God for
Christ's sake hath forgiven you.
EPHESIANS 4:31-32

Wrath is cruel, and anger is outrageous;
but who is able to stand before envy?
PROVERBS 27:4

If thine enemy be hungry, give him
bread to eat; and if he be thirsty,
give him water to drink: For thou shalt
heap coals of fire upon his head,
and the LORD shall reward thee.
PROVERBS 25:21-22

But now ye also put off all these;
anger, wrath, malice, blasphemy, filthy
communication out of your mouth.
COLOSSIANS 3:8

Dearly beloved, avenge not yourselves, but rather give place unto wrath: for it is written, Vengeance is mine; I will repay, saith the Lord. Therefore if thine enemy hunger, feed him; if he thirst, give him drink: for in so doing thou shalt heap coals of fire on his head. Be not overcome of evil, but overcome evil with good.
Romans 12:19–21

BELIEF

For God so loved the world, that
he gave his only begotten Son, that
whosoever believeth in him should
not perish, but have everlasting life.
JOHN 3:16

> To him give all the prophets witness,
> that through his name whosoever
> believeth in him shall receive
> remission of sins.
> ACTS 10:43

As it is written, Behold, I lay in Sion a
stumblingstone and rock of offence:
and whosoever believeth on him
shall not be ashamed.
ROMANS 9:33

> But as many as received him,
> to them gave he power to become
> the sons of God, even to them that
> believe on his name.
> JOHN 1:12

He that believeth on him is not
condemned: but he that believeth
not is condemned already, because
he hath not believed in the name
of the only begotten Son of God.
JOHN 3:18

> He that believeth on the Son hath
> everlasting life: and he that believeth
> not the Son shall not see life; but the
> wrath of God abideth on him.
> JOHN 3:36

Wherefore also it is contained in the
scripture, Behold, I lay in Sion a chief
corner stone, elect, precious:
and he that believeth on him
shall not be confounded.
1 PETER 2:6

> And they said, Believe on the Lord
> Jesus Christ, and thou shalt be
> saved, and thy house.
> ACTS 16:31

I am come a light into the world,
that whosoever believeth on me
should not abide in darkness.
JOHN 12:46

> And Jesus said unto them, I am the
> bread of life: he that cometh to me
> shall never hunger; and he that
> believeth on me shall never thirst.
> JOHN 6:35

Jesus said unto him, If thou
canst believe, all things are
possible to him that believeth.
MARK 9:23

> Jesus saith unto him, Thomas,
> because thou hast seen me, thou
> hast believed: blessed are they that
> have not seen, and yet have believed.
> JOHN 20:29

Verily, verily, I say unto you, He that
believeth on me hath everlasting life.
JOHN 6:47

CHARITY

Blessed is he that considereth the
poor: the LORD will deliver him in
time of trouble. The LORD will
preserve him, and keep him alive;
and he shall be blessed upon the
earth: and thou wilt not deliver him
unto the will of his enemies.
PSALM 41:1–2

He that hath pity upon the poor
lendeth unto the LORD; and that which
he hath given will he pay him again.
PROVERBS 19:17

But when thou makest a feast,
call the poor, the maimed, the lame,
the blind: And thou shalt be blessed;
for they cannot recompense thee:
for thou shalt be recompensed at
the resurrection of the just.
LUKE 14:13–14

Sell that ye have, and give alms;
provide yourselves bags which wax
not old, a treasure in the heavens
that faileth not, where no thief
approacheth, neither moth corrupteth.
LUKE 12:33

He that despiseth his neighbour
sinneth: but he that hath mercy
on the poor, happy is he.
PROVERBS 14:21

Give, and it shall be given unto you;
good measure, pressed down, and
shaken together, and running over,
shall men give into your bosom. For
with the same measure that ye mete
withal it shall be measured to you again.
LUKE 6:38

He hath dispersed, he hath given
to the poor; his righteousness
endureth for ever; his horn shall
be exalted with honour.
PSALM 112:9

And now abideth faith, hope,
charity, these three; but the
greatest of these is charity.
1 CORINTHIANS 13:13

He that giveth unto the poor shall
not lack: but he that hideth his
eyes shall have many a curse.
PROVERBS 28:27

Every man according as he
purposeth in his heart, so let him
give; not grudgingly, or of necessity:
for God loveth a cheerful giver.
2 CORINTHIANS 9:7

There is that scattereth, and yet
increaseth; and there is that withholdeth
more than is meet, but it tendeth to
poverty. The liberal soul shall be made
fat: and he that watereth shall be
watered also himself.
PROVERBS 11:24–25

I have been young, and now am old;
yet have I not seen the righteous
forsaken, nor his seed begging bread.
PSALM 37:25

Charge them that are rich in this world,
that they be not highminded, nor trust
in uncertain riches, but in the living
God, who giveth us richly all things to
enjoy; That they do good, that they be
rich in good works, ready to distribute,
willing to communicate.
1 TIMOTHY 6:17–18

Cast thy bread upon the waters:
for thou shalt find it after many days.
ECCLESIASTES 11:1

And if thou draw out thy soul to the
hungry, and satisfy the afflicted soul;
then shall thy light rise in obscurity,
and thy darkness be as the noon day.
ISAIAH 58:10

Is it not to deal thy bread to the
hungry, and that thou bring the poor
that are cast out to thy house? when
thou seest the naked, that thou cover
him; and that thou hide not thyself
from thine own flesh? Then shall thy
light break forth as the morning,
and thine health shall spring forth
speedily: and thy righteousness shall
go before thee; the glory of the
LORD shall be thy reward.
ISAIAH 58:7–8

And the Levite, (because he hath no
part nor inheritance with thee,)
and the stranger, and the fatherless,
and the widow, which are within thy
gates, shall come, and shall eat and be
satisfied; that the LORD thy God may
bless thee in all the work of thine hand
which thou doest.
DEUTERONOMY 14:29

Then Jesus beholding him loved him,
and said unto him, One thing thou
lackest: go thy way, sell whatsoever
thou hast, and give to the poor, and
thou shalt have treasure in heaven: and
come, take up the cross, and follow me.
MARK 10:21

He is ever merciful, and lendeth;
and his seed is blessed.
PSALM 37:26

CHILDREN

And they said, Believe on the Lord
Jesus Christ, and thou shalt be saved,
and thy house.
ACTS 16:31

For the promise is unto you,
and to your children, and to all
that are afar off, even as many
as the LORD our God shall call.
ACTS 2:39

And all thy children shall be taught
of the LORD; and great shall be the
peace of thy children.
ISAIAH 54:13

For I will pour water upon him that is
thirsty, and floods upon the dry ground:
I will pour my spirit upon thy seed, and
my blessing upon thine offspring.
ISAIAH 44:3

Thy wife shall be as a fruitful vine by
the sides of thine house: thy children
like olive plants round about thy table.
PSALM 128:3

Yet setteth he the poor on high
from affliction, and maketh him
families like a flock.
PSALM 107:41

Children's children are the crown
of old men; and the glory of
children are their fathers.
PROVERBS 17:6

Lo, children are an heritage of the LORD: and the fruit of the womb is his reward. As arrows are in the hand of a mighty man; so are children of the youth. Happy is the man that hath his quiver full of them: they shall not be ashamed, but they shall speak with the enemies in the gate.

PSALM 127:3–5

CHILDREN'S DUTIES

Children, obey your parents in the
Lord: for this is right. Honour thy
father and mother; which is the first
commandment with promise; That
it may be well with thee, and thou
mayest live long on the earth.
EPHESIANS 6:1–3

> Children, obey your parents
> in all things: for this is well
> pleasing unto the Lord.
> COLOSSIANS 3:20

Honour thy father
and thy mother.
LUKE 18:20

> Cursed be he that setteth light
> by his father or his mother.
> DEUTERONOMY 27:16

Ye shall fear every man
his mother, and his father.
LEVITICUS 19:3

> My son, if thine heart be wise,
> my heart shall rejoice, even mine.
> Yea, my reins shall rejoice, when
> thy lips speak right things.
> PROVERBS 23:15–16

My son, keep thy father's
commandment, and forsake
not the law of thy mother.
PROVERBS 6:20

Honour thy father and thy
mother, as the Lord thy God
hath commanded thee.
DEUTERONOMY 5:16

A wise son heareth his father's
instruction: but a scorner
heareth not rebuke.
PROVERBS 13:1

My son, if sinners entice
thee, consent thou not.
PROVERBS 1:10

A fool despiseth his father's
instruction: but he that
regardeth reproof is prudent.
PROVERBS 15:5

Even a child is known by his
doings, whether his work be
pure, and whether it be right.
PROVERBS 20:11

A wise son maketh a glad father:
but a foolish son is the heaviness
of his mother.
PROVERBS 10:1

Whoso keepeth the law is a wise son:
but he that is a companion of riotous
men shameth his father.
PROVERBS 28:7

Now therefore hearken unto me,
O ye children: for blessed are they
that keep my ways. Hear instruction,
and be wise, and refuse it not.
PROVERBS 8:32–33

Hearken unto thy father that
begat thee, and despise not
thy mother when she is old.
PROVERBS 23:22

The father of the righteous shall greatly
rejoice: and he that begetteth a wise
child shall have joy of him. Thy father
and thy mother shall be glad, and she
that bare thee shall rejoice. My son,
give me thine heart, and let thine
eyes observe my ways.
PROVERBS 23:24–26

COMFORT

God is our refuge and strength, a very
present help in trouble. Therefore
will not we fear, though the earth be
removed, and though the mountains
be carried into the midst of the sea;
Though the waters thereof roar and be
troubled, though the mountains shake
with the swelling thereof.
PSALM 46:1–3

Though I walk in the midst of trouble,
thou wilt revive me: thou shalt stretch
forth thine hand against the wrath
of mine enemies, and thy right
hand shall save me.
PSALM 138:7

The LORD is my rock, and my fortress,
and my deliverer; my God, my
strength, in whom I will trust; my
buckler, and the horn of my salvation,
and my high tower.
PSALM 18:2

For he hath not despised nor abhorred
the affliction of the afflicted;
neither hath he hid his face from him;
but when he cried unto him, he heard.
PSALM 22:24

Though he fall, he shall not be utterly
cast down: for the LORD upholdeth
him with his hand.
PSALM 37:24

The LORD is good, a strong hold in the
day of trouble; and he knoweth them
that trust in him.
NAHUM 1:7

But the salvation of the righteous
is of the LORD: he is their strength
in the time of trouble.
PSALM 37:39

Cast thy burden upon the LORD,
and he shall sustain thee: he shall never
suffer the righteous to be moved.
PSALM 55:22

These things I have spoken unto you,
that in me ye might have peace.
In the world ye shall have tribulation:
but be of good cheer; I have overcome
the world.
JOHN 16:33

Come unto me, all ye that labour and
are heavy laden, and I will give you rest.
MATTHEW 11:28

For the Lord will not cast off for ever:
But though he cause grief, yet will
he have compassion according to the
multitude of his mercies. For he doth
not afflict willingly nor grieve the
children of men.
LAMENTATIONS 3:31–33

For as the sufferings of Christ
abound in us, so our consolation
also aboundeth by Christ.
2 CORINTHIANS 1:5

The Lord also will be a refuge for the oppressed, a refuge in times of trouble.
Psalm 9:9

Wait on the Lord: be of good courage, and he shall strengthen thine heart: wait, I say, on the Lord.
Psalm 27:14

CONTENTMENT

A merry heart doeth good like a
medicine: but a broken spirit
drieth the bones.
PROVERBS 17:22

Let your conversation be without
covetousness; and be content with
such things as ye have: for he hath said,
I will never leave thee, nor forsake thee.
HEBREWS 13:5

All the days of the afflicted are evil:
but he that is of a merry heart hath a
continual feast.
PROVERBS 15:15

A sound heart is the life of the flesh:
but envy the rottenness of the bones.
PROVERBS 14:30

But godliness with contentment
is great gain.
1 TIMOTHY 6:6

Let not thine heart envy sinners: but be
thou in the fear of the LORD all the day
long. For surely there is an end; and
thine expectation shall not be cut off.
PROVERBS 23:17–18

CORRECTION, GOD'S

For whom the LORD loveth he
correcteth; even as a father the
son in whom he delighteth.
PROVERBS 3:12

Thou shalt also consider in thine
heart, that, as a man chasteneth his
son, so the LORD thy God chasteneth
thee. Therefore thou shalt keep the
commandments of the LORD thy God,
to walk in his ways, and to fear him.
DEUTERONOMY 8:5–6

Blessed is the man whom thou
chastenest, O LORD, and teachest him
out of thy law; That thou mayest give
him rest from the days of adversity,
until the pit be digged for the wicked.
PSALM 94:12–13

For whom the Lord loveth he
chasteneth, and scourgeth every
son whom he receiveth. If ye endure
chastening, God dealeth with you as
with sons; for what son is he whom the
father chasteneth not?
HEBREWS 12:6–7

But when we are judged, we are
chastened of the Lord, that we should
not be condemned with the world.
I CORINTHIANS 11:32

For which cause we faint not; but though our outward man perish, yet the inward man is renewed day by day. For our light affliction, which is but for a moment, worketh for us a far more exceeding and eternal weight of glory.

2 CORINTHIANS 4:16–17

COURAGE

Wait on the LORD: be of good courage,
and he shall strengthen thine heart:
wait, I say, on the LORD.
PSALM 27:14

> For the LORD loveth judgment,
> and forsaketh not his saints;
> they are preserved for ever: but the
> seed of the wicked shall be cut off.
> PSALM 37:28

But now thus saith the LORD that
created thee, O Jacob, and he that
formed thee, O Israel, Fear not: for
I have redeemed thee, I have called
thee by thy name: thou art mine.
ISAIAH 43:1

> Fear not: for they that be with us
> are more than they that be with them.
> 2 KINGS 6:16

Trust in the LORD, and do good;
so shalt thou dwell in the land,
and verily thou shalt be fed.
PSALM 37:3

> He giveth power to the faint;
> and to them that have no might he
> increaseth strength.
> ISAIAH 40:29

Be of good courage, and he shall
strengthen your heart, all ye
that hope in the LORD.
PSALM 31:24

I know both how to be abased, and I know how to abound: every where and in all things I am instructed both to be full and to be hungry, both to abound and to suffer need. I can do all things through Christ which strengtheneth me.

PHILIPPIANS 4:12–13

DEATH

Yea, though I walk through the valley
of the shadow of death, I will fear
no evil: for thou art with me; thy rod
and thy staff they comfort me.
PSALM 23:4

> O death, where is thy sting?
> O grave, where is thy victory?
> 1 CORINTHIANS 15:55

The wicked is driven away in
his wickedness: but the righteous
hath hope in his death.
PROVERBS 14:32

> Much more then, being now
> justified by his blood, we shall be
> saved from wrath through him.
> ROMANS 5:9

Verily, verily, I say unto you,
If a man keep my saying,
he shall never see death.
JOHN 8:51

> I will ransom them from the power of
> the grave; I will redeem them from
> death: O death, I will be thy plagues;
> O grave, I will be thy destruction:
> repentance shall be hid from mine eyes.
> HOSEA 13:14

For this God is our God for ever
and ever: he will be our guide
even unto death.
PSALM 48:14

But God will redeem my soul
from the power of the grave:
for he shall receive me.
PSALM 49:15

My flesh and my heart faileth:
but God is the strength of my heart,
and my portion for ever.
PSALM 73:26

He will swallow up death in victory;
and the Lord God will wipe away
tears from off all faces.
ISAIAH 25:8

Precious in the sight of the LORD
is the death of his saints.
PSALM 116:15

Mark the perfect man, and behold
the upright: for the end of
that man is peace.
PSALM 37:37

But though our outward man
perish, yet the inward man is
renewed day by day.
2 CORINTHIANS 4:16

That whosoever believeth in him should
not perish, but have eternal life.
JOHN 3:15

For I am persuaded, that neither death,
nor life, nor angels, nor principalities,
nor powers, nor things present, nor
things to come, Nor height, nor depth,
nor any other creature, shall be able
to separate us from the love of God,
which is in Christ Jesus our Lord.
ROMANS 8:38–39

ENEMIES

And the LORD shall help them, and deliver them: he shall deliver them from the wicked, and save them, because they trust in him.
PSALM 37:40

The LORD hath sworn by his right hand, and by the arm of his strength, Surely I will no more give thy corn to be meat for thine enemies; and the sons of the stranger shall not drink thy wine, for the which thou hast laboured.
ISAIAH 62:8

For the rod of the wicked shall not rest upon the lot of the righteous; lest the righteous put their hands unto iniquity.
PSALM 125:3

His heart is established, he shall not be afraid, until he see his desire upon his enemies.
PSALM 112:8

Thy right hand, O LORD, is become glorious in power: thy right hand, O LORD, hath dashed in pieces the enemy.
EXODUS 15:6

Through God we shall do valiantly: for he it is that shall tread down our enemies.
PSALM 60:12

No weapon that is formed against thee
shall prosper; and every tongue that
shall rise against thee in judgment
thou shalt condemn. This is the heritage
of the servants of the LORD, and their
righteousness is of me, saith the LORD.
ISAIAH 54:17

When a man's ways please the LORD,
he maketh even his enemies to
be at peace with him.
PROVERBS 16:7

The LORD taketh my part with them
that help me: therefore shall I see my
desire upon them that hate me.
PSALM 118:7

That he would grant unto us, that we
being delivered out of the hand of our
enemies might serve him without fear.
LUKE 1:74

The LORD shall cause thine enemies
that rise up against thee to be smitten
before thy face: they shall come out
against thee one way, and flee before
thee seven ways.
DEUTERONOMY 28:7

For the LORD your God is he that goeth
with you, to fight for you against
your enemies, to save you.
DEUTERONOMY 20:4

And shall not God avenge his own
elect, which cry day and night unto
him, though he bear long with them?
LUKE 18:7

Behold, they shall surely gather
together, but not by me: whosoever
shall gather together against thee
shall fall for thy sake.
ISAIAH 54:15

Ye that love the LORD, hate evil:
he preserveth the souls of his saints;
he delivereth them out of the hand
of the wicked.
PSALM 97:10

But I will deliver thee in that day, saith
the LORD: and thou shalt not be given
into the hand of the men of whom thou
art afraid. For I will surely deliver thee,
and thou shalt not fall by the sword,
but thy life shall be for a prey unto
thee: because thou hast put thy trust
in me, saith the LORD.
JEREMIAH 39:17–18

But the LORD your God ye shall fear;
and he shall deliver you out of the
hand of all your enemies.
2 KINGS 17:39

And he answered, Fear not:
for they that be with us are more
than they that be with them.
2 KINGS 6:16

Be not afraid of sudden fear, neither
of the desolation of the wicked, when
it cometh. For the LORD shall be thy
confidence, and shall keep thy foot
from being taken.
PROVERBS 3:25–26

That we should be saved
from our enemies, and from
the hand of all that hate us.
LUKE 1:71

For I am with thee, and no man
shall set on thee to hurt thee: for
I have much people in this city.
ACTS 18:10

So that we may boldly say, The Lord
is my helper, and I will not fear
what man shall do unto me.
HEBREWS 13:6

ETERNAL LIFE

Verily, verily I say unto you, He that believeth on me hath everlasting life.
JOHN 6:47

Jesus said unto her, I am the resurrection, and the life: he that believeth in me, though he were dead, yet shall he live: And whosoever liveth and believeth in me shall never die. Believest thou this?
JOHN 11:25–26

And this is the promise that he hath promised us, even eternal life.
1 JOHN 2:25

For the Lord himself shall descend from heaven with a shout, with the voice of the archangel, and with the trump of God: and the dead in Christ shall rise first.
1 THESSALONIANS 4:16

For since by man came death, by man came also the resurrection of the dead.
1 CORINTHIANS 15:21

For the wages of sin is death; but the gift of God is eternal life through Jesus Christ our Lord.
ROMANS 6:23

For God so loved the world, that he gave his only begotten Son, that whosoever believeth in him should not perish, but have everlasting life.
JOHN 3:16

Marvel not at this: for the hour is
coming, in the which all that are in the
graves shall hear his voice, And shall
come forth; they that have done good,
unto the resurrection of life; and
they that have done evil, unto the
resurrection of damnation.
JOHN 5:28–29

These things have I written unto you
that believe on the name of the Son of
God; that ye may know that ye have
eternal life, and that ye may believe on
the name of the Son of God.
1 JOHN 5:13

So also is the resurrection of the dead.
It is sown in corruption; it is raised in
incorruption: It is sown in dishonour;
it is raised in glory: it is sown in
weakness; it is raised in power: It is
sown a natural body; it is raised a
spiritual body. There is a natural body,
and there is a spiritual body.
1 CORINTHIANS 15:42–44

But if the Spirit of him that raised up
Jesus from the dead dwell in you,
he that raised up Christ from the dead
shall also quicken your mortal bodies
by his Spirit that dwelleth in you.
ROMANS 8:11

For thou wilt not leave my soul in hell;
neither wilt thou suffer thine Holy
One to see corruption.
PSALM 16:10

And God shall wipe away all tears
from their eyes; and there shall be no
more death, neither sorrow, nor crying,
neither shall there be any more pain:
for the former things are passed away.
REVELATION 21:4

And though after my skin worms
destroy this body, yet in my flesh
shall I see God: Whom I shall see for
myself, and mine eyes shall behold,
and not another; though my reins
be consumed within me.
JOB 19:26–27

For he that soweth to his flesh shall
of the flesh reap corruption; but he
that soweth to the Spirit shall of the
Spirit reap life everlasting.
GALATIANS 6:8

For we know that if our earthly
house of this tabernacle were
dissolved, we have a building of
God, an house not made with
hands, eternal in the heavens.
2 CORINTHIANS 5:1

And many of them that sleep in the
dust of the earth shall awake, some to
everlasting life, and some to shame
and everlasting contempt.
DANIEL 12:2

And this is the record, that God
hath given to us eternal life,
and this life is in his Son.
1 JOHN 5:11

Thy dead men shall live, together with
my dead body shall they arise.
Awake and sing, ye that dwell in dust:
for thy dew is as the dew of herbs, and
the earth shall cast out the dead.
ISAIAH 26:19

But is now made manifest by the
appearing of our Saviour Jesus Christ,
who hath abolished death, and hath
brought life and immortality to light
through the gospel.
2 TIMOTHY 1:10

In my Father's house are many mansions:
if it were not so, I would have told you.
I go to prepare a place for you. And if
I go and prepare a place for you, I will
come again, and receive you unto myself;
that where I am, there ye may be also.
JOHN 14:2–3

FAITH

Now faith is the substance of
things hoped for, the evidence
of things not seen.
HEBREWS 11:1

> Watch ye, stand fast in the faith,
> quit you like men, be strong.
> 1 CORINTHIANS 16:13

If any of you lack wisdom, let him ask
of God, that giveth to all men liberally,
and upbraideth not; and it shall be
given him. But let him ask in faith,
nothing wavering. For he that wavereth
is like a wave of the sea driven with the
wind and tossed.
JAMES 1:5–6

> As ye have therefore received
> Christ Jesus the Lord, so walk ye
> in him: Rooted and built up in
> him, and stablished in the faith,
> as ye have been taught, abounding
> therein with thanksgiving.
> COLOSSIANS 2:6–7

For by grace are ye saved through
faith; and that not of yourselves:
it is the gift of God.
EPHESIANS 2:8

> For ye are all the children of
> God by faith in Christ Jesus.
> GALATIANS 3:26

The fruit of the Spirit is love, joy, peace, longsuffering, gentleness, goodness, faith, meekness, temperance: against such there is no law.
GALATIANS 5:22–23

But continue thou in the things which thou hast learned and hast been assured of, knowing of whom thou hast learned them; And that from a child thou hast known the holy scriptures, which are able to make thee wise unto salvation through faith which is in Christ Jesus.
2 TIMOTHY 3:14–15

For we walk by faith, not by sight.
2 CORINTHIANS 5:7

And Jesus answering saith unto them, Have faith in God. For verily I say unto you, That whosoever shall say unto this mountain, Be thou removed, and be thou cast into the sea; and shall not doubt in his heart, but shall believe that those things which he saith shall come to pass; he shall have whatsoever he saith.
MARK 11:22–23

He that cometh to God must believe that he is, and that he is a rewarder of them that diligently seek him.
HEBREWS 11:6

I am crucified with Christ: nevertheless I live; yet not I, but Christ liveth in me: and the life which I now live in the flesh I live by the faith of the Son of God, who loved me, and gave himself for me.
GALATIANS 2:20

FAITHFULNESS, GOD'S

Know therefore that the LORD
thy God, he is God, the faithful
God, which keepeth covenant
and mercy with them that love
him and keep his commandments
to a thousand generations.
DEUTERONOMY 7:9

(For the LORD thy God is a merciful
God;) he will not forsake thee,
neither destroy thee, nor forget the
covenant of thy fathers which
he sware unto them.
DEUTERONOMY 4:31

He hath remembered his covenant for
ever, the word which he commanded
to a thousand generations.
PSALM 105:8

God is not a man, that he should lie;
neither the son of man, that he should
repent: hath he said, and shall he not
do it? or hath he spoken, and shall
he not make it good?
NUMBERS 23:19

Let us hold fast the profession
of our faith without wavering;
(for he is faithful that promised;).
HEBREWS 10:23

If we believe not, yet he abideth
faithful: he cannot deny himself.
2 TIMOTHY 2:13

The Lord is not slack concerning his
promise, as some men count slackness;
but is longsuffering to us-ward.
2 PETER 3:9

Blessed be the LORD, that hath
given rest unto his people Israel,
according to all that he promised:
there hath not failed one word
of all his good promise.
1 KINGS 8:56

O Lord, thou art my God;
I will exalt thee, I will praise
thy name; for thou hast done
wonderful things; thy counsels
of old are faithfulness and truth.
ISAIAH 25:1

And they that know thy name will put
their trust in thee: for thou, LORD, hast
not forsaken them that seek thee.
PSALM 9:10

Thy word is true from the beginning:
and every one of thy righteous
judgments endureth for ever.
PSALM 119:160

For ever, O LORD, thy word is settled
in heaven. Thy faithfulness is
unto all generations.
PSALM 119:89–90

And also the Strength of Israel
will not lie nor repent: for he is
not a man, that he should repent.
1 SAMUEL 15:29

For all the promises of God in
him are yea, and in him Amen,
unto the glory of God by us.
2 CORINTHIANS 1:20

My covenant will I not break, nor alter
the thing that is gone out of my lips.
PSALM 89:34

FEAR

And he said unto them, Why are ye so fearful? how is it that ye have no faith?
MARK 4:40

Fear not, little flock; for it is your Father's good pleasure to give you the kingdom.
LUKE 12:32

For I the LORD thy God will hold thy right hand, saying unto thee, Fear not; I will help thee.
ISAIAH 41:13

But whoso hearkeneth unto me shall dwell safely, and shall be quiet from fear of evil.
PROVERBS 1:33

And fear not them which kill the body, but are not able to kill the soul.
MATTHEW 10:28

Be not afraid of sudden fear, neither of the desolation of the wicked, when it cometh. For the LORD shall be thy confidence, and shall keep thy foot from being taken.
PROVERBS 3:25–26

For God hath not given us the spirit of fear; but of power, and of love, and of a sound mind.
2 TIMOTHY 1:7

The LORD shall give thee rest
from thy sorrow, and from thy fear,
and from the hard bondage wherein
thou wast made to serve.
ISAIAH 14:3

When thou liest down, thou shalt
not be afraid: yea, thou shalt lie down,
and thy sleep shall be sweet.
PROVERBS 3:24

In righteousness shalt thou be
established: thou shalt be far
from oppression; for thou shalt
not fear: and from terror; for it
shall not come near thee.
ISAIAH 54:14

For ye have not received the spirit of
bondage again to fear; but ye have
received the Spirit of adoption,
whereby we cry, Abba, Father.
ROMANS 8:15

So that we may boldly say, The Lord
is my helper, and I will not fear
what man shall do unto me.
HEBREWS 13:6

God is our refuge and strength,
a very present help in trouble.
PSALM 46:1

The fear of man bringeth a snare:
but whoso putteth his trust in
the Lord shall be safe.
PROVERBS 29:25

I, even I, am he that comforteth you:
who art thou, that thou shouldest be
afraid of a man that shall die, and of the
son of man which shall be made as grass.
ISAIAH 51:12

Fear not; for thou shalt not be
ashamed: neither be thou confounded.
ISAIAH 54:4

When thou passest through the waters,
I will be with thee; and through the
rivers, they shall not overflow thee:
when thou walkest through the fire,
thou shalt not be burned; neither shall
the flame kindle upon thee.
ISAIAH 43:2

Peace I leave with you, my peace I
give unto you: not as the world giveth,
give I unto you. Let not your heart be
troubled, neither let it be afraid.
JOHN 14:27

FOOD AND CLOTHING

And ye shall eat in plenty, and be
satisfied, and praise the name of
the LORD your God, that hath dealt
wondrously with you: and my people
shall never be ashamed.
JOEL 2:26

He maketh peace in thy borders, and
filleth thee with the finest of the wheat.
PSALM 147:14

He hath given meat unto them
that fear him: he will ever be
mindful of his covenant.
PSALM 111:5

The righteous eateth to the
satisfying of his soul: but the
belly of the wicked shall want.
PROVERBS 13:25

I will abundantly bless her provision:
I will satisfy her poor with bread.
PSALM 132:15

Therefore take no thought, saying,
What shall we eat? or, What shall
we drink? or, Wherewithal shall we
be clothed? (For after all these
things do the Gentiles seek:) for your
heavenly Father knoweth that ye
have need of all these things.
MATTHEW 6:31-32

FORGIVENESS

And when ye stand praying, forgive, if ye
have ought against any: that your Father
also which is in heaven may forgive you
your trespasses. But if ye do not forgive,
neither will your Father which is in
heaven forgive your trespasses.
MARK 11:25–26

> For if ye forgive men their
> trespasses, your heavenly
> Father will also forgive you.
> MATTHEW 6:14

Therefore if thine enemy hunger,
feed him; if he thirst, give him drink.
ROMANS 12:20

FRUITFULNESS

I am the true vine, and my father is the
husbandman. Every branch in me that
beareth not fruit he taketh away:
and every branch that beareth fruit, he
purgeth it, that it may bring forth more
fruit. Now ye are clean through the
word which I have spoken unto you.
Abide in me, and I in you. As the
branch cannot bear fruit of itself,
except it abide in the vine; no more
can ye, except ye abide in me. I am
the vine, ye are the branches: He that
abideth in me, and I in him, the same
bringeth forth much fruit: for without
me ye can do nothing.
JOHN 15:1–5

> And he shall be like a tree planted
> by the rivers of water, that bringeth
> forth his fruit in his season; his leaf
> also shall not wither; and whatsoever
> he doeth shall prosper.
> PSALM 1:3

Therefore they shall come and sing
in the height of Zion, and shall flow
together to the goodness of the LORD,
for wheat, and for wine, and for oil,
and for the young of the flock and
of the herd: and their soul shall be as
a watered garden; and they shall not
sorrow any more at all.
JEREMIAH 31:12

They shall still bring forth fruit in old
age; they shall be fat and flourishing.
PSALM 92:14

I will be as the dew unto Israel:
he shall grow as the lily, and cast
forth his roots as Lebanon.
HOSEA 14:5

For if these things be in you, and
abound, they make you that ye shall
neither be barren nor unfruitful in the
knowledge of our Lord Jesus Christ.
2 PETER 1:8

GOSSIP

Thou shalt not go up and down as a talebearer among thy people: neither shalt thou stand against the blood of thy neighbour: I am the LORD.
LEVITICUS 19:16

> The words of a talebearer are as wounds, and they go down into the innermost parts of the belly.
> PROVERBS 18:8

He that goeth about as a talebearer revealeth secrets: therefore meddle not with him that flattereth with his lips.
PROVERBS 20:19

> A talebearer revealeth secrets: but he that is of a faithful spirit concealeth the matter.
> PROVERBS 11:13

Where no wood is, there the fire goeth out: so where there is no talebearer, the strife ceaseth. As coals are to burning coals, and wood to fire; so is a contentious man to kindle strife. The words of a talebearer are as wounds, and they go down into the innermost parts of the belly.
PROVERBS 26:20–22

> A froward man soweth strife: and a whisperer separateth chief friends.
> PROVERBS 16:28

The tongue deviseth mischiefs; like a
sharp razor, working deceitfully.
PSALM 52:2

The north wind driveth away rain:
so doth an angry countenance a
backbiting tongue.
PROVERBS 25:23

Keep thy tongue from evil,
and thy lips from speaking guile.
PSALM 34:13

GRACE, GROWTH IN

Herein is my Father glorified,
that ye bear much fruit;
so shall ye be my disciples.
JOHN 15:8

> And this I pray, that your love may
> abound yet more and more in
> knowledge and in all judgment.
> PHILIPPIANS 1:9

Being filled with the fruits of
righteousness, which are by Jesus Christ,
unto the glory and praise of God.
PHILIPPIANS 1:11

> But we all, with open face beholding
> as in a glass the glory of the Lord,
> are changed into the same image
> from glory to glory, even as by
> the Spirit of the Lord.
> 2 CORINTHIANS 3:18

The LORD will perfect that which
concerneth me: thy mercy, O LORD,
endureth for ever: forsake not the
works of thine own hands.
PSALM 138:8

> But the path of the just is as the
> shining light, that shineth more and
> more unto the perfect day.
> PROVERBS 4:18

And beside this, giving all diligence,
add to your faith virtue; and to
virtue knowledge.
2 PETER 1:5

The righteous also shall hold on his
way, and he that hath clean hands
shall be stronger and stronger.
Job 17:9

Which is come unto you, as it is in all
the world; and bringeth forth fruit, as
it doth also in you, since the day ye
heard of it, and knew the grace of
God in truth.
COLOSSIANS 1:6

I press toward the mark for the prize of
the high calling of God in Christ Jesus.
Let us therefore, as many as be
perfect, be thus minded: and if in
any thing ye be otherwise minded,
God shall reveal even this unto you.
Nevertheless, whereto we have already
attained, let us walk by the same rule,
let us mind the same thing.
PHILIPPIANS 3:14–16

Furthermore then we beseech you,
brethren, and exhort you by the Lord
Jesus, that as ye have received of us how
ye ought to walk and to please God,
so ye would abound more and more.
1 THESSALONIANS 4:1

We are bound to thank God always for
you, brethren, as it is meet, because
that your faith groweth exceedingly,
and the charity of every one of you all
toward each other aboundeth.
2 THESSALONIANS 1:3

GUIDANCE

And thine ears shall hear a word behind
thee, saying, This is the way, walk ye in
it, when ye turn to the right hand, and
when ye turn to the left.
ISAIAH 30:21

For this God is our God for
ever and ever: he will be our
guide even unto death.
PSALM 48:14

A man's heart deviseth his way:
but the LORD directeth his steps.
PROVERBS 16:9

The steps of a good man are
ordered by the LORD: and he
delighteth in his way.
PSALM 37:23

For his God doth instruct him to
discretion, and doth teach him.
ISAIAH 28:26

And I will bring the blind by a way that
they knew not; I will lead them in paths
that they have not known: I will make
darkness light before them, and crooked
things straight. These things will I do
unto them, and not forsake them.
ISAIAH 42:16

In all thy ways acknowledge him,
and he shall direct thy paths.
PROVERBS 3:6

The righteousness of the perfect shall direct his way: but the wicked shall fall by his own wickedness.

PROVERBS 11:5

GUILT

If we confess our sins, he is faithful
and just to forgive us our sins, and to
cleanse us from all unrighteousness.
1 JOHN 1:9

> Let the wicked forsake his way, and
> the unrighteous man his thoughts:
> and let him return unto the LORD, and
> he will have mercy upon him; and to
> our God, for he will abundantly pardon.
> ISAIAH 55:7

For the LORD your God is gracious and
merciful, and will not turn away his
face from you, if ye return unto him.
2 CHRONICLES 30:9

> As far as the east is from the west,
> so far hath he removed our
> transgressions from us.
> PSALM 103:12

For if our heart condemn us,
God is greater than our heart,
and knoweth all things.
1 JOHN 3:20

> For I will be merciful to their
> unrighteousness, and their sins and
> their iniquities will I remember no more.
> HEBREWS 8:12

Therefore if any man be in Christ,
he is a new creature: old things
are passed away; behold, all things
are become new.
2 CORINTHIANS 5:17

For I will forgive their iniquity,
and I will remember their sin no more.
JEREMIAH 31:34

And I will cleanse them from all their
iniquity, whereby they have sinned
against me; and I will pardon all their
iniquities, whereby they have sinned,
and whereby they have transgressed
against me.
JEREMIAH 33:8

I write unto you, little children,
because your sins are forgiven
you for his name's sake.
1 JOHN 2:12

I, even I, am he that blotteth out
thy transgressions for mine own sake,
and will not remember thy sins.
ISAIAH 43:25

But if we walk in the light, as he is in
the light, we have fellowship one with
another, and the blood of Jesus Christ
his Son cleanseth us from all sin.
1 JOHN 1:7

HELP IN TROUBLES

But the salvation of the righteous
is of the LORD: he is their strength
in the time of trouble.
PSALM 37:39

The LORD openeth the eyes of the blind:
the LORD raiseth them that are bowed
down: the LORD loveth the righteous.
PSALM 146:8

The LORD is good, a strong hold
in the day of trouble; and he
knoweth them that trust in him.
NAHUM 1:7

Though he fall, he shall not be
utterly cast down: for the LORD
upholdeth him with his hand.
PSALM 37:24

Thou art my hiding place; thou shalt
preserve me from trouble; thou shalt
compass me about with songs of
deliverance.
PSALM 32:7

Thou, which hast shewed me great
and sore troubles, shalt quicken me
again, and shalt bring me up again
from the depths of the earth.
PSALM 71:20

Why art thou cast down, O my soul?
and why art thou disquieted within
me? hope thou in God: for I shall yet
praise him, who is the health of my
countenance, and my God.
PSALM 42:11

My flesh and my heart faileth:
but God is the strength of my
heart, and my portion for ever.
PSALM 73:26

There shall no evil befall thee,
neither shall any plague come
nigh thy dwelling. For he shall
give his angels charge over thee,
to keep thee in all thy ways.
PSALM 91:10–11

They that sow in tears shall reap in joy.
He that goeth forth and weepeth,
bearing precious seed, shall doubtless
come again with rejoicing, bringing
his sheaves with him.
PSALM 126:5–6

Though I walk in the midst of trouble,
thou wilt revive me: thou shalt stretch
forth thine hand against the wrath of
mine enemies, and thy right hand
shall save me.
PSALM 138:7

O love the LORD, all ye his saints: for
the LORD preserveth the faithful, and
plentifully rewardeth the proud doer.
PSALM 31:23

Though ye have lien among the pots,
yet shall ye be as the wings of a dove
covered with silver, and her feathers
with yellow gold.
PSALM 68:13

The LORD is my strength and my shield;
my heart trusted in him, and I am helped:
therefore my heart greatly rejoiceth;
and with my song will I praise him.

PSALM 28:7

The LORD also will be a refuge for the
oppressed, a refuge in times of trouble.
PSALM 9:9

For he hath not despised nor abhorred
the affliction of the afflicted; neither
hath he hid his face from him; but
when he cried unto him, he heard.

PSALM 22:24

Many are the afflictions of the
righteous: but the LORD delivereth
him out of them all.
PSALM 34:19

For the LORD will not cast off for ever:
But though he cause grief, yet will he
have compassion according to the
multitude of his mercies. For he doth
not afflict willingly nor grieve the
children of men.

LAMENTATIONS 3:31–33

The LORD is my rock, and my fortress,
and my deliverer; my God, my strength,
in whom I will trust; my buckler,
and the horn of my salvation,
and my high tower.
PSALM 18:2

Rejoice not against me, O mine enemy:
when I fall, I shall arise; when I sit in
darkness, the LORD shall be a light unto
me. I will bear the indignation of the
LORD, because I have sinned against
him, until he plead my cause, and
execute judgment for me: he will bring
me forth to the light, and I shall behold
his righteousness.
MICAH 7:8–9

These things I have spoken unto you,
that in me ye might have peace.
In the world ye shall have tribulation:
but be of good cheer; I have
overcome the world.
JOHN 16:33

HOLY SPIRIT

Behold, I will pour out my spirit
unto you, I will make known
my words unto you.
PROVERBS 1:23

> And I will pray the Father, and he
> shall give you another Comforter,
> that he may abide with you for ever;
> Even the Spirit of truth; whom the
> world cannot receive, because it seeth
> him not, neither knoweth him: but ye
> know him; for he dwelleth with you,
> and shall be in you.
> JOHN 14:16–17

He that believeth on me, as the
scripture hath said, out of his belly
shall flow rivers of living water. (But
this spake he of the Spirit, which they
that believe on him should receive:
for the Holy Ghost was not yet given;
because that Jesus was not yet glorified.)
JOHN 7:38–39

> Howbeit when he, the Spirit of truth,
> is come, he will guide you into all truth:
> for he shall not speak of himself;
> but whatsoever he shall hear,
> that shall he speak: and he will
> shew you things to come.
> JOHN 16:13

If ye then, being evil, know how to
give good gifts unto your children:
how much more shall your heavenly
Father give the Holy Spirit to them
that ask him?
LUKE 11:13

But whosoever drinketh of the water
that I shall give him shall never thirst;
but the water that I shall give him shall
be in him a well of water springing up
into everlasting life.
JOHN 4:14

And I will put my spirit within you,
and cause you to walk in my statutes,
and ye shall keep my judgments,
and do them.
EZEKIEL 36:27

That the blessing of Abraham might
come on the Gentiles through Jesus
Christ; that we might receive the
promise of the Spirit through faith.
GALATIANS 3:14

But the anointing which ye have
received of him abideth in you, and
ye need not that any man teach you:
but as the same anointing teacheth you
of all things, and is truth, and is no lie,
and even as it hath taught you,
ye shall abide in him.
1 JOHN 2:27

For the kingdom of God is not meat
and drink; but righteousness, and
peace, and joy in the Holy Ghost.
ROMANS 14:17

For ye have not received the spirit of
bondage again to fear; but ye have
received the Spirit of adoption, whereby
we cry, Abba, Father.
ROMANS 8:15

HONESTY

Ye shall not steal, neither deal falsely,
neither lie one to another.
LEVITICUS 19:11

Are there yet the treasures of
wickedness in the house of the wicked,
and the scant measure that is
abominable? Shall I count them pure
with the wicked balances, and with the
bag of deceitful weights? For the rich
men thereof are full of violence,
and the inhabitants thereof have
spoken lies, and their tongue is
deceitful in their mouth.
MICAH 6:10–12

Ye shall do no unrighteousness in
judgment, in meteyard, in weight,
or in measure.
LEVITICUS 19:35

A false balance is abomination to the
LORD: but a just weight is his delight.
PROVERBS 11:1

Withhold not good from them to
whom it is due, when it is in the
power of thine hand to do it.
PROVERBS 3:27

And if thou sell ought unto thy
neighbour, or buyest ought of thy
neighbour's hand, ye shall not
oppress one another.
LEVITICUS 25:14

Ye shall not therefore oppress one
another; but thou shalt fear thy God:
for I am the LORD your God.
LEVITICUS 25:17

But thou shalt have a perfect and just
weight, a perfect and just measure
shalt thou have: that thy days may be
lengthened in the land which the LORD
thy God giveth thee. For all that do such
things, and all that do unrighteously, are
an abomination unto the LORD thy God.
DEUTERONOMY 25:15–16

That no man go beyond and defraud
his brother in any matter: because that
the Lord is the avenger of all such,
as we also have forewarned you and
testified. For God hath not called us
unto uncleanness, but unto holiness.
1 THESSALONIANS 4:6–7

The wicked borroweth, and payeth
not again: but the righteous
sheweth mercy, and giveth.
PSALM 37:21

Lie not one to another, seeing that
ye have put off the old man with his
deeds; And have put on the new man,
which is renewed in knowledge
after the image of him that created him.
COLOSSIANS 3:9–10

Better is a little with righteousness
than great revenues without right.
PROVERBS 16:8

He that walketh righteously, and
speaketh uprightly; he that despiseth
the gain of oppressions, that shaketh
his hands from holding of bribes,
that stoppeth his ears from hearing
of blood, and shutteth his eyes from
seeing evil; He shall dwell on high:
his place of defence shall be the
munitions of rocks: bread shall be
given him; his waters shall be sure.
ISAIAH 33:15–16

HOPE

Why art thou cast down, O my soul? and why art thou disquieted within me? hope thou in God: for I shall yet praise him, who is the health of my countenance, and my God.
PSALM 42:11

Who by him do believe in God, that raised him up from the dead, and gave him glory; that your faith and hope might be in God.
1 PETER 1:21

Wherefore gird up the loins of your mind, be sober, and hope to the end for the grace that is to be brought unto you at the revelation of Jesus Christ.
1 PETER 1:13

And every man that hath this hope in him purifieth himself, even as he is pure.
1 JOHN 3:3

The wicked is driven away in his wickedness: but the righteous hath hope in his death.
PROVERBS 14:32

For the hope which is laid up for you in heaven, whereof ye heard before in the word of the truth of the gospel.
COLOSSIANS 1:5

Which is Christ in you,
the hope of glory.
Colossians 1:27

> Be of good courage, and he
> shall strengthen your heart,
> all ye that hope in the Lord.
> Psalm 31:24

For thou art my hope, O Lord God:
thou art my trust from my youth.
Psalm 71:5

> Blessed be the God and Father
> of our Lord Jesus Christ, which
> according to his abundant mercy
> hath begotten us again unto a
> lively hope by the resurrection of
> Jesus Christ from the dead.
> 1 Peter 1:3

HOSPITALITY

Use hospitality one to another without grudging. As every man hath received the gift, even so minister the same one to another, as good stewards of the manifold grace of God.
1 PETER 4:9–10

If a brother or sister be naked, and destitute of daily food, And one of you say unto them, Depart in peace, be ye warmed and filled; notwithstanding ye give them not those things which are needful to the body; what doth it profit?
JAMES 2:15-16

For whosoever shall give you a cup of water to drink in my name, because ye belong to Christ, verily I say unto you, he shall not lose his reward.
MARK 9:41

I have shewed you all things, how that so labouring ye ought to support the weak, and to remember the words of the Lord Jesus, how he said, It is more blessed to give than to receive.
ACTS 20:35

Be not forgetful to entertain strangers: for thereby some have entertained angels unawares.
HEBREWS 13:2

But whoso hath this world's good,
and seeth his brother have need,
and shutteth up his bowels
of compassion from him, how
dwelleth the love of God in him?
1 JOHN 3:17

And the King shall answer and say
unto them, Verily I say unto you,
Inasmuch as ye have done it unto one
of the least of these my brethren,
ye have done it unto me.
MATTHEW 25:40

For I mean not that other men be eased,
and ye burdened: But by an equality,
that now at this time your abundance
may be a supply for their want, that their
abundance also may be a supply for
your want: that there may be equality.
2 CORINTHIANS 8:13-14

Distributing to the necessity of
saints; given to hospitality.
ROMANS 12:13

For I was an hungred, and ye gave
me meat: I was thirsty, and ye gave
me drink: I was a stranger, and ye took
me in: Naked, and ye clothed me:
I was sick, and ye visited me: I was in
prison, and ye came unto me.
MATTHEW 25:35-36

HUMILITY

Whosoever therefore shall humble himself as this little child, the same is greatest in the kingdom of heaven.
MATTHEW 18:4

> LORD, thou hast heard the desire of the humble: thou wilt prepare their heart, thou wilt cause thine ear to hear.
> PSALM 10:17

And whosoever shall exalt himself shall be abased; and he that shall humble himself shall be exalted.
MATTHEW 23:12

> For thus saith the high and lofty One that inhabiteth eternity, whose name is Holy; I dwell in the high and holy place, with him also that is of a contrite and humble spirit, to revive the spirit of the humble, and to revive the heart of the contrite ones.
> ISAIAH 57:15

When he maketh inquisition for blood, he remembereth them: he forgetteth not the cry of the humble.
PSALM 9:12

> Better it is to be of an humble spirit with the lowly, than to divide the spoil with the proud.
> PROVERBS 16:19

But he giveth more grace. Wherefore
he saith, God resisteth the proud,
but giveth grace unto the humble.
JAMES 4:6

By humility and the fear of the LORD
are riches, and honour, and life.
PROVERBS 22:4

Surely he scorneth the scorners:
but he giveth grace unto the lowly.
PROVERBS 3:34

The fear of the LORD is the instruction of
wisdom; and before honour is humility.
PROVERBS 15:33

A man's pride shall bring him low:
but honour shall uphold the
humble in spirit.
PROVERBS 29:23

Humble yourselves therefore
under the mighty hand of God,
that he may exalt you in due time.
1 PETER 5:6

JOY

For ye shall go out with joy, and be led forth with peace: the mountains and the hills shall break forth before you into singing, and all the trees of the field shall clap their hands.
ISAIAH 55:12

> Blessed is the people that know the joyful sound: they shall walk, O LORD, in the light of thy countenance. In thy name shall they rejoice all the day: and in thy righteousness shall they be exalted.
> PSALM 89:15–16

The voice of rejoicing and salvation is in the tabernacles of the righteous: the right hand of the LORD doeth valiantly.
PSALM 118:15

> Thou hast put gladness in my heart, more than in the time that their corn and their wine increased.
> PSALM 4:7

They that sow in tears shall reap in joy. He that goeth forth and weepeth, bearing precious seed, shall doubtless come again with rejoicing, bringing his sheaves with him.
PSALM 126:5–6

> These things have I spoken unto you, that my joy might remain in you, and that your joy might be full.
> JOHN 15:11

Thou wilt shew me the path of life:
in thy presence is fulness of joy;
at thy right hand there are pleasures
for evermore.
PSALM 16:11

Light is sown for the righteous, and
gladness for the upright in heart.
Rejoice in the LORD, ye righteous;
and give thanks at the remembrance
of his holiness.
PSALM 97:11–12

Yet I will rejoice in the LORD, I will
joy in the God of my salvation.
HABAKKUK 3:18

Therefore the redeemed of the LORD
shall return, and come with singing
unto Zion; and everlasting joy shall
be upon their head: they shall obtain
gladness and joy; and sorrow and
mourning shall flee away.
ISAIAH 51:11

For our heart shall rejoice in him,
because we have trusted in
his holy name.
PSALM 33:21

Then he said unto them, Go your way,
eat the fat, and drink the sweet, and
send portions unto them for whom
nothing is prepared: for this day is holy
unto our LORD: neither be ye sorry; for
the joy of the LORD is your strength.
NEHEMIAH 8:10

And thou shalt rejoice in the
LORD, and shalt glory in the
Holy One of Israel.
ISAIAH 41:16

Whom having not seen, ye love; in
whom, though now ye see him not,
yet believing, ye rejoice with joy
unspeakable and full of glory.
1 PETER 1:8

I will greatly rejoice in the LORD, my
soul shall be joyful in my God; for he
hath clothed me with the garments of
salvation, he hath covered me with the
robe of righteousness, as a bridegroom
decketh himself with ornaments, and as
a bride adorneth herself with her jewels.
ISAIAH 61:10

The righteous shall be glad in the
LORD, and shall trust in him; and
all the upright in heart shall glory.
PSALM 64:10

My soul shall be satisfied as with
marrow and fatness; and my mouth
shall praise thee with joyful lips.
PSALM 63:5

But let the righteous be glad;
let them rejoice before God:
yea, let them exceedingly rejoice.
PSALM 68:3

I will see you again, and your
heart shall rejoice, and your joy
no man taketh from you.
JOHN 16:22

LAZINESS

And that ye study to be quiet, and
to do your own business, and to
work with your own hands, as we
commanded you; That ye may walk
honestly toward them that are without,
and that ye may have lack of nothing.
1 THESSALONIANS 4:11–12

Not slothful in business; fervent
in spirit; serving the Lord.
ROMANS 12:11

He that tilleth his land shall have plenty
of bread: but he that followeth after
vain persons shall have poverty enough.
PROVERBS 28:19

The soul of the sluggard desireth,
and hath nothing: but the soul of
the diligent shall be made fat.
PROVERBS 13:4

He becometh poor that dealeth
with a slack hand: but the hand of
the diligent maketh rich. He that
gathereth in summer is a wise son:
but he that sleepeth in harvest is
a son that causeth shame.
PROVERBS 10:4–5

Much food is in the tillage of the
poor: but there is that is destroyed
for want of judgment.
PROVERBS 13:23

The husbandman that laboureth
must be first partaker of the fruits.
2 TIMOTHY 2:6

For even when we were with you,
this we commanded you, that if
any would not work, neither should
he eat. For we hear that there are
some which walk among you
disorderly, working not at all, but are
busybodies. Now them that are such
we command and exhort by our Lord
Jesus Christ, that with quietness they
work, and eat their own bread.
2 THESSALONIANS 3:10–12

Love not sleep, lest thou come to
poverty; open thine eyes, and thou
shalt be satisfied with bread.
PROVERBS 20:13

The way of the slothful man is as
an hedge of thorns: but the way
of the righteous is made plain.
PROVERBS 15:19

Be thou diligent to know the state of
thy flocks, and look well to thy herds.
PROVERBS 27:23

The thoughts of the diligent tend
only to plenteousness; but of every
one that is hasty only to want.
PROVERBS 21:5

The hand of the diligent shall bear rule:
but the slothful shall be under tribute.
PROVERBS 12:24

Let him that stole steal no more: but rather let him labour, working with his hands the thing which is good, that he may have to give to him that needeth.

EPHESIANS 4:28

He that tilleth his land shall be satisfied with bread: but he that followeth vain persons is void of understanding.

PROVERBS 12:11

And thou shalt have goats' milk enough for thy food, for the food of thy household, and for the maintenance for thy maidens.

PROVERBS 27:27

LONELINESS

I will not leave you comfortless:
I will come to you.
JOHN 14:18

> Then shalt thou call, and the
> LORD shall answer; thou shalt cry,
> and he shall say, Here I am.
> ISAIAH 58:9

Since thou wast precious in my
sight, thou hast been honourable,
and I have loved thee.
ISAIAH 43:4

> And will be a Father unto you,
> and ye shall be my sons and
> daughters, saith the Lord Almighty.
> 2 CORINTHIANS 6:18

And, behold, I am with thee, and will
keep thee in all places whither thou
goest, and will bring thee again into
this land; for I will not leave thee,
until I have done that which I have
spoken to thee of.
GENESIS 28:15

> And ye are complete in him,
> which is the the head of all
> principality and power.
> COLOSSIANS 2:10

But I am poor and needy; yet the
Lord thinketh upon me: thou art
my help and my deliverer; make
no tarrying, O my God.
PSALM 40:17

LONG LIFE

And even to your old age I am he;
and even to hoar hairs will I carry
you: I have made, and I will bear;
even I will carry, and will deliver you.
ISAIAH 46:4

With the ancient is wisdom; and in
length of days understanding.
With him is wisdom and strength, he
hath counsel and understanding.
JOB 12:12–13

The glory of young men is their
strength: and the beauty of old
men is the grey head.
PROVERBS 20:29

Children's children are the crown
of old men; and the glory of
children are their fathers.
PROVERBS 17:6

The hoary head is a crown of glory, if it
be found in the way of righteousness.
PROVERBS 16:31

And thine age shall be clearer than
the noonday: thou shalt shine forth,
thou shalt be as the morning.
JOB 11:17

My son, forget not my law; but let
thine heart keep my commandments:
For length of days, and long life,
and peace, shall they add to thee.
PROVERBS 3:1–2

Cast me not off in the time
of old age; forsake me not
when my strength faileth.
PSALM 71:9

O God, thou hast taught me from my
youth: and hitherto have I declared
thy wondrous works. Now also when
I am old and greyheaded, O God,
forsake me not; until I have shewed thy
strength unto this generation, and thy
power to every one that is to come.
PSALM 71:17–18

LORD, make me to know mine end,
and the measure of my days, what
it is: that I may know how frail I am.
Behold, thou hast made my days as
an handbreadth; and mine age is as
nothing before thee.
PSALM 39:4-5

Ye shall walk in all the ways which the
LORD your God hath commanded you,
that ye may live, and that it may be well
with you, and that ye may prolong your
days in the land which ye shall possess.
DEUTERONOMY 5:33

With long life will I satisfy him,
and shew him my salvation.
PSALM 91:16

For by me thy days shall be
multiplied, and the years of
thy life shall be increased.
PROVERBS 9:11

The fear of the LORD prolongeth days: but the years of the wicked shall be shortened.
PROVERBS 10:27

That thou mightest fear the LORD thy God, to keep all his statutes and his commandments, which I command thee, thou, and thy son, and thy son's son, all the days of thy life; and that thy days may be prolonged.
DEUTERONOMY 6:2

LOVE, BROTHERLY

A new commandment I give unto you,
That ye love one another; as I have loved
you, that ye also love one another. By
this shall all men know that ye are my
disciples, if ye have love one to another.
JOHN 13:34–35

Let love be without dissimulation.
Abhor that which is evil; cleave to that
which is good. Be kindly affectioned
one to another with brotherly love; in
honour preferring one another.
ROMANS 12:9-10

But as touching brotherly love ye
need not that I write unto you:
for ye yourselves are taught of
God to love one another.
I THESSALONIANS 4:9

He that loveth his brother abideth
in the light, and there is none
occasion of stumbling in him.
1 JOHN 2:10

Seeing ye have purified your souls in
obeying the truth through the Spirit
unto unfeigned love of the brethren,
see that ye love one another with
a pure heart fervently.
I PETER 1:22

My little children, let us not
love in word, neither in tongue;
but in deed and in truth.
1 JOHN 3:18

Beloved, if God so loved us,
we ought also to love one another.
1 JOHN 4:11

> Beloved, let us love one another:
> for love is of God; and every one
> that loveth is born of God, and
> knoweth God. He that loveth not
> knoweth not God; for God is love.
> 1 JOHN 4:7–8

Put on therefore, as the elect of God,
holy and beloved, bowels of mercies,
kindness, humbleness of mind,
meekness, longsuffering; Forbearing
one another, and forgiving one
another, if any man have a quarrel
against any: even as Christ forgave
you, so also do ye.
COLOSSIANS 3:12–13

LOVE, GOD'S

For God so loved the world, that
he gave his only begotten Son, that
whosoever believeth in him should not
perish, but have everlasting life.
JOHN 3:16

And he will love thee, and bless thee,
and multiply thee: he will also bless the
fruit of thy womb, and the fruit of thy
land, thy corn, and thy wine, and thine
oil, the increase of thy kine, and the
flocks of thy sheep, in the land which
he sware unto thy fathers to give thee.
DEUTERONOMY 7:13

The LORD openeth the eyes of the
blind: the LORD raiseth them that
are bowed down: the LORD loveth
the righteous.
PSALM 146:8

The way of the wicked is an
abomination unto the LORD:
but he loveth him that followeth
after righteousness.
PROVERBS 15:9

For the Father himself loveth you,
because ye have loved me, and have
believed that I came out from God.
JOHN 16:27

For as a young man marrieth a virgin,
so shall thy sons marry thee: and as the
bridegroom rejoiceth over the bride,
so shall thy God rejoice over thee.
ISAIAH 62:5

Herein is love, not that we loved God, but that he loved us, and sent his Son to be the propitiation for our sins.
1 JOHN 4:10

I will heal their backsliding, I will love them freely: for mine anger is turned away from him.
HOSEA 14:4

The LORD thy God in the midst of thee is mighty; he will save, he will rejoice over thee with joy; he will rest in his love, he will joy over thee with singing.
ZEPHANIAH 3:17

The LORD hath appeared of old unto me, saying, Yea, I have loved thee with an everlasting love: therefore with lovingkindness have I drawn thee.
JEREMIAH 31:3

Yea, I will rejoice over them to do them good, and I will plant them in this land assuredly with my whole heart and with my whole soul.
JEREMIAH 32:41

And we have known and believed the love that God hath to us. God is love; and he that dwelleth in love dwelleth in God, and God in him.
1 JOHN 4:16

We love him, because he first loved us.
1 JOHN 4:19

And I have declared unto them thy name, and will declare it: that the love wherewith thou hast loved me may be in them, and I in them.
JOHN 17:26

I in them, and thou in me, that they may be made perfect in one; and that the world may know that thou hast sent me, and hast loved them, as thou hast loved me.
JOHN 17:23

Now our Lord Jesus Christ himself, and God, even our Father, which hath loved us, and hath given us everlasting consolation and good hope through grace, Comfort your hearts, and stablish you in every good word and work.
2 THESSALONIANS 2:16–17

LOVING GOD

Know therefore that the LORD
thy God, he is God, the faithful
God, which keepeth covenant and
mercy with them that love him
and keep his commandments to a
thousand generations.
DEUTERONOMY 7:9

> I love them that love me; and those
> that seek me early shall find me.
> PROVERBS 8:17

He that hath my commandments,
and keepeth them, he it is that loveth
me: and he that loveth me shall be
loved of my Father, and I will love him,
and will manifest myself to him.
JOHN 14:21

> That I may cause those that
> love me to inherit substance;
> and I will fill their treasures.
> PROVERBS 8:21

But as it is written, Eye hath not seen,
nor ear heard, neither have entered into
the heart of man, the things which God
hath prepared for them that love him.
1 CORINTHIANS 2:9

> Delight thyself also in the LORD:
> and he shall give thee the desires
> of thine heart.
> PSALM 37:4

Because he hath set his love upon
me, therefore will I deliver him:
I will set him on high, because
he hath known my name.
PSALM 91:14

The LORD preserveth all them that love
him: but all the wicked will he destroy.
PSALM 145:20

Grace be with all them that love our
Lord Jesus Christ in sincerity. Amen.
EPHESIANS 6:24

LUST

For all that is in the world, the lust of the flesh, and the lust of the eyes, and the pride of life, is not of the Father, but is of the world. And the world passeth away, and the lust thereof: but he that doeth the will of God abideth for ever.
1 JOHN 2:16–17

Ye have heard that it was said by them of old time, Thou shalt not commit adultery: But I say unto you, That whosoever looketh on a woman to lust after her hath committed adultery with her already in his heart.
MATTHEW 5:27–28

Lust not after her beauty in thine heart; neither let her take thee with her eyelids. For by means of a whorish woman a man is brought to a piece of bread: and the adultress will hunt for the precious life. Can a man take fire in his bosom, and his clothes not be burned? Can one go upon hot coals, and his feet not be burned? So he that goeth in to his neighbour's wife; whosoever toucheth her shall not be innocent.
PROVERBS 6:25–29

Submit yourselves therefore to God. Resist the devil, and he will flee from you. Draw nigh to God, and he will draw nigh to you. Cleanse your hands, ye sinners; and purify your hearts, ye double minded.
JAMES 4:7-8

Dearly beloved, I beseech you as strangers and pilgrims, abstain from fleshly lusts, which war against the soul.
1 PETER 2:11

As obedient children, not fashioning yourselves according to the former lusts in your ignorance: But as he which hath called you is holy, so be ye holy in all manner of conversation; Because it is written, Be ye holy; for I am holy.
1 PETER 1:14–16

Whereby are given unto us exceeding great and precious promises: that by these ye might be partakers of the divine nature, having escaped the corruption that is in the world through lust.
2 PETER 1:4

And they that are Christ's have crucified the flesh with the affections and lusts.
GALATIANS 5:24

For we ourselves also were sometimes foolish, disobedient, deceived, serving divers lusts and pleasures, living in malice and envy, hateful, and hating one another. But after that the kindness and love of God our Saviour toward man appeared, Not by works of righteousness which we have done, but according to his mercy he saved us, by the washing of regeneration, and renewing of the Holy Ghost.
TITUS 3:3–5

For the grace of God that bringeth
salvation hath appeared to all men,
Teaching us that, denying ungodliness
and worldly lusts, we should live
soberly, righteously, and godly,
in this present world.
TITUS 2:11–12

Flee also youthful lusts: but follow
righteousness, faith, charity, peace,
with them that call on the Lord
out of a pure heart.
2 TIMOTHY 2:22

Walk in the Spirit, and ye shall not fulfil
the lust of the flesh. For the flesh lusteth
against the Spirit, and the Spirit against
the flesh: and these are contrary the one
to the other: so that ye cannot do the
things that ye would.
GALATIANS 5:16–17

Likewise reckon ye also yourselves to
be dead indeed unto sin, but alive unto
God through Jesus Christ our Lord.
Let not sin therefore reign in your
mortal body, that ye should obey it in
the lusts thereof. . . . For sin shall not
have dominion over you: for ye are not
under the law, but under grace.
ROMANS 6:11–12, 14

But put ye on the Lord Jesus Christ,
and make not provision for the flesh,
to fulfil the lusts thereof.
ROMANS 13:14

LYING

Lie not one to another, seeing that
ye have put off the old man with his
deeds; And have put on the new man,
which is renewed in knowledge after
the image of him that created him.
COLOSSIANS 3:9–10

And ye shall not swear by my name
falsely, neither shalt thou profane the
name of thy God: I am the LORD.
LEVITICUS 19:12

A man that beareth false witness
against his neighbour is a maul,
and a sword, and a sharp arrow.
PROVERBS 25:18

A faithful witness will not lie:
but a false witness will utter lies.
PROVERBS 14:5

Thou shalt not raise a false report:
put not thine hand with the wicked
to be an unrighteous witness.
EXODUS 23:1

A false witness shall not
be unpunished, and he that
speaketh lies shall not escape.
PROVERBS 19:5

Be not a witness against thy
neighbour without cause;
and deceive not with thy lips.
PROVERBS 24:28

The wicked are estranged from the
womb: they go astray as soon as
they be born, speaking lies.
PSALM 58:3

But the fearful, and unbelieving,
and the abominable, and murderers,
and whoremongers, and sorcerers, and
idolaters, and all liars, shall have their
part in the lake which burneth with
fire and brimstone: which is
the second death.
REVELATION 21:8

A false witness shall not be
unpunished, and he that
speaketh lies shall perish.
PROVERBS 19:9

But if ye have bitter envying and
strife in your hearts, glory not,
and lie not against the truth.
JAMES 3:14

The lip of truth shall be established
for ever: but a lying tongue
is but for a moment.
PROVERBS 12:19

MARRIAGE

Live joyfully with the wife whom
thou lovest all the days of the life
of thy vanity, which he hath given
thee under the sun, all the days of
thy vanity: for that is thy portion
in this life, and in thy labour which
thou takest under the sun.
ECCLESIASTES 9:9

Drink waters out of thine
own cistern, and running
waters out of thine own well.
PROVERBS 5:15

Let the husband render unto the
wife due benevolence: and likewise
also the wife unto the husband.
1 CORINTHIANS 7:3

Wives, submit yourselves unto
your own husbands, as unto the
Lord. For the husband is the head
of the wife, even as Christ is the
head of the church: and he is
the saviour of the body.
EPHESIANS 5:22-23

Husbands, love your wives,
even as Christ also loved the
church, and gave himself for it.
EPHESIANS 5:25

Let thy fountain be blessed: and rejoice
with the wife of thy youth. Let her be
as the loving hind and pleasant roe; let
her breasts satisfy thee at all times; and
be thou ravished always with her love.
And why wilt thou, my son, be ravished
with a strange woman, and embrace
the bosom of a stranger?
PROVERBS 5:18–20

So ought men to love their wives
as their own bodies. He that
loveth his wife loveth himself.
EPHESIANS 5:28

For this cause shall a man leave
his father and mother, and shall
be joined unto his wife, and they
two shall be one flesh.
EPHESIANS 5:31

Nevertheless let every one of you in
particular so love his wife even as
himself; and the wife see that she
reverence her husband.
EPHESIANS 5:33

But if any provide not for his own,
and specially for those of his own
house, he hath denied the faith,
and is worse than an infidel.
1 TIMOTHY 5:8

Wives, submit yourselves unto your
own husbands, as it is fit in the
Lord. Husbands, love your wives,
and be not bitter against them.
COLOSSIANS 3:18–19

Likewise, ye husbands, dwell with them according to knowledge, giving honour unto the wife, as unto the weaker vessel, and as being heirs together of the grace of life; that your prayers be not hindered.

1 PETER 3:7

That they may teach the young women to be sober, to love their husbands, to love their children, To be discreet, chaste, keepers at home, good, obedient to their own husbands, that the word of God be not blasphemed.

TITUS 2:4–5

MEEKNESS

Blessed are the meek: for
they shall inherit the earth.
MATTHEW 5:5

> But with righteousness shall he
> judge the poor, and reprove with
> equity for the meek of the earth.
> ISAIAH 11:4

The meek also shall increase their joy
in the LORD, and the poor among men
shall rejoice in the Holy One of Israel.
ISAIAH 29:19

> The LORD lifteth up the meek:
> he casteth the wicked
> down to the ground.
> PSALM 147:6

The meek will he guide in judgment:
and the meek will he teach his way.
PSALM 25:9

> But the meek shall inherit the earth;
> and shall delight themselves in the
> abundance of peace.
> PSALM 37:11

A soft answer turneth away wrath:
but grievous words stir up anger.
PROVERBS 15:1

> The meek shall eat and be satisfied:
> they shall praise the LORD that seek
> him: your heart shall live for ever.
> PSALM 22:26

But let it be the hidden man of the
heart, in that which is not corruptible,
even the ornament of a meek and
quiet spirit, which is in the sight of
God of great price.
1 PETER 3:4

Seek ye the LORD, all ye meek of
the earth, which have wrought his
judgment; seek righteousness, seek
meekness: it may be ye shall be hid
in the day of the LORD's anger.
ZEPHANIAH 2:3

For the LORD taketh pleasure in
his people: he will beautify the
meek with salvation.
PSALM 149:4

MERCY

And therefore will the LORD wait,
that he may be gracious unto you,
and therefore will he be exalted, that
he may have mercy upon you: for the
LORD is a God of judgment: blessed
are all they that wait for him.
ISAIAH 30:18

And the LORD passed by before
him, and proclaimed, The LORD, The
LORD God, merciful and gracious,
longsuffering, and abundant in
goodness and truth, Keeping mercy
for thousands, forgiving iniquity and
transgression and sin, and that will
by no means clear the guilty; visiting
the iniquity of the fathers upon the
children, and upon the children's
children, unto the third and to the
fourth generation.
EXODUS 34:6–7

Like as a father pitieth his children, so
the LORD pitieth them that fear him.
PSALM 103:13

But the mercy of the LORD is from
everlasting to everlasting upon them
that fear him, and his righteousness
unto children's children.
PSALM 103:17

For in my wrath I smote thee, but in
my favour have I had mercy on thee.
ISAIAH 60:10

For my name's sake will I defer mine
anger, and for my praise will I refrain
for thee, that I cut thee not off.
ISAIAH 48:9

And he said, I will make all my
goodness pass before thee, and I will
proclaim the name of the LORD before
thee; and will be gracious to whom I
will be gracious, and will shew mercy
on whom I will shew mercy.
EXODUS 33:19

And I will have mercy upon her
that had not obtained mercy;
and I will say to them which were
not my people, Thou art my people;
and they shall say, Thou art my God.
HOSEA 2:23

MONEY

Labour not to be rich: cease from thine own wisdom. Wilt thou set thine eyes upon that which is not? for riches certainly make themselves wings; they fly away as an eagle toward heaven.
PROVERBS 23:4–5

A little that a righteous man hath is better than the riches of many wicked.
PSALM 37:16

Hearken, my beloved brethren,
Hath not God chosen the poor
of this world rich in faith, and
heirs of the kingdom which he hath
promised to them that love him?
JAMES 2:5

Better is an handful with quietness, than both the hands full with travail and vexation of spirit.
ECCLESIASTES 4:6

But thou shalt remember the LORD thy God: for it is he that giveth thee power to get wealth, that he may establish his covenant which he sware unto thy fathers, as it is this day.
DEUTERONOMY 8:18

For the oppression of the poor, for the sighing of the needy, now will I arise, saith the LORD; I will set him in safety from him that puffeth at him.
PSALM 12:5

Whoso mocketh the poor reproacheth his Maker: and he that is glad at calamities shall not be unpunished.
PROVERBS 17:5

Both riches and honour come of thee, and thou reignest over all; and in thine hand is power and might; and in thine hand it is to make great, and to give strength unto all.
1 CHRONICLES 29:12

Rob not the poor, because he is poor: neither oppress the afflicted in the gate.
PROVERBS 22:22

Charge them that are rich in this world, that they be not highminded, nor trust in uncertain riches, but in the living God, who giveth us richly all things to enjoy; That they do good, that they be rich in good works, ready to distribute, willing to communicate; Laying up in store for themselves a good foundation against the time to come, that they may lay hold on eternal life.
1 TIMOTHY 6:17–19

The sleep of a labouring man is sweet, whether he eat little or much: but the abundance of the rich will not suffer him to sleep. There is a sore evil which I have seen under the sun, namely, riches kept for the owners thereof to their hurt. But those riches perish by evil travail: and he begetteth a son, and there is nothing in his hand.
ECCLESIASTES 5:12–14

Better is little with the fear
of the LORD than great treasure
and trouble therewith.
PROVERBS 15:16

The rich and poor meet together:
the LORD is the maker of them all.
PROVERBS 22:2

For the needy shall not always be
forgotten: the expectation of the
poor shall not perish for ever.
PSALM 9:18

He that trusteth in his riches
shall fall; but the righteous
shall flourish as a branch.
PROVERBS 11:28

A faithful man shall abound with
blessings: but he that maketh haste
to be rich shall not be innocent.
PROVERBS 28:20

Riches profit not in the day
of wrath: but righteousness
delivereth from death.
PROVERBS 11:4

They shall cast their silver in the streets,
and their gold shall be removed: their
silver and their gold shall not be able
to deliver them in the day of the wrath
of the LORD: they shall not satisfy their
souls, neither fill their bowels: because it
is the stumblingblock of their iniquity.
EZEKIEL 7:19

There is that maketh himself rich, yet
hath nothing: there is that maketh
himself poor, yet hath great riches.
PROVERBS 13:7

He that loveth silver shall not be
satisfied with silver; nor he that
loveth abundance with increase:
this is also vanity.
ECCLESIASTES 5:10

He that oppresseth the poor to increase
his riches, and he that giveth to the
rich, shall surely come to want.
PROVERBS 22:16

He that hasteth to be rich hath an
evil eye, and considereth not that
poverty shall come upon him.
PROVERBS 28:22

For we brought nothing into
this world, and it is certain
we can carry nothing out.
1 TIMOTHY 6:7

Better is the poor that walketh in his
uprightness, than he that is perverse
in his ways, though he be rich.
PROVERBS 28:6

Blessed is he that considereth
the poor: the LORD will deliver
him in time of trouble.
PSALM 41:1

OBEDIENCE

See, I have set before thee this day life
and good, and death and evil; In that
I command thee this day to love the
LORD thy God, to walk in his ways,
and to keep his commandments and his
statutes and his judgments, that thou
mayest live and multiply: and the LORD
thy God shall bless thee in the land
whither thou goest to possess it.
DEUTERONOMY 30:15–16

And thou shalt do that which is
right and good in the sight of the
LORD: that it may be well with thee,
and that thou mayest go in and
possess the good land which the
LORD sware unto thy fathers.
DEUTERONOMY 6:18

Hear therefore, O Israel, and observe
to do it; that it may be well with thee,
and that ye may increase mightily,
as the LORD God of thy fathers hath
promised thee, in the land that
floweth with milk and honey.
DEUTERONOMY 6:3

Keep therefore the words of this
covenant, and do them, that ye
may prosper in all that ye do.
DEUTERONOMY 29:9

If ye know these things,
happy are ye if ye do them.
JOHN 13:17

Whosoever therefore shall break
one of these least commandments,
and shall teach men so, he shall be
called the least in the kingdom of
heaven: but whosoever shall do and
teach them, the same shall be called
great in the kingdom of heaven.
MATTHEW 5:19

Wherefore it shall come to pass,
if ye hearken to these judgments,
and keep, and do them, that the
LORD thy God shall keep unto thee
the covenant and the mercy which
he sware unto thy fathers.
DEUTERONOMY 7:12

O that there were such an heart in
them, that they would fear me, and
keep all my commandments always,
that it might be well with them,
and with their children for ever!
DEUTERONOMY 5:29

Those things, which ye have both
learned, and received, and heard,
and seen in me, do: and the God
of peace shall be with you.
PHILIPPIANS 4:9

Therefore whosoever heareth these
sayings of mine, and doeth them,
I will liken him unto a wise man,
which built his house upon a rock:
And the rain descended, and the
floods came, and the winds blew,
and beat upon that house; and it fell
not: for it was founded upon a rock.
MATTHEW 7:24–25

Jesus answered and said unto him,
If a man love me, he will keep my
words: and my Father will love
him, and we will come unto him,
and make our abode with him.
JOHN 14:23

And we know that all things work
together for good to them that love
God, to them who are the called
according to his purpose.
ROMANS 8:28

If ye keep my commandments,
ye shall abide in my love; even as I
have kept my Father's commandments,
and abide in his love.
JOHN 15:10

For not the hearers of the law are
just before God, but the doers
of the law shall be justified.
ROMANS 2:13

Verily, verily, I say unto you, He that
heareth my word, and believeth on him
that sent me, hath everlasting life, and
shall not come into condemnation;
but is passed from death unto life.
JOHN 5:24

But whoso looketh into the perfect
law of liberty, and continueth therein,
he being not a forgetful hearer,
but a doer of the work, this man
shall be blessed in his deed.
JAMES 1:25

For whosoever shall do the will of my Father which is in heaven, the same is my brother, and sister, and mother.
MATTHEW 12:50

And the world passeth away, and the lust thereof: but he that doeth thewill of God abideth for ever.
1 JOHN 2:17

Not every one that saith unto me, Lord, Lord, shall enter into the kingdom of heaven; but he that doeth the will of my Father which is in heaven.
MATTHEW 7:21

And whatsoever we ask, we receive of him, because we keep his commandments, and do those things that are pleasing in his sight.
1 JOHN 3:22

PARENTS' DUTIES

For I know him, that he will command
his children and his household after
him, and they shall keep the way of the
LORD, to do justice and judgment.
GENESIS 18:19

And thou shalt shew thy son in that
day, saying, This is done because
of that which the LORD did unto me
when I came forth out of Egypt.
EXODUS 13:8

And, ye fathers, provoke not your
children to wrath: but bring them
up in the nurture and admonition
of the Lord.
EPHESIANS 6:4

Fathers, provoke not your children
to anger, lest they be discouraged.
COLOSSIANS 3:21

Train up a child in the way he
should go: and when he is old,
he will not depart from it.
PROVERBS 22:6

Correct thy son, and he shall
give thee rest; yea, he shall
give delight unto thy soul.
PROVERBS 29:17

And ye shall teach them your children, speaking of them when thou sittest in thine house, and when thou walkest by the way, when thou liest down, and when thou risest up.
DEUTERONOMY 11:19

Only take heed to thyself, and keep thy soul diligently, lest thou forget the things which thine eyes have seen, and lest they depart from thy heart all the days of thy life: but teach them thy sons, and thy sons' sons. . .Gather me the people together, and I will make them hear my words, that they may learn to fear me all the days that they shall live upon the earth, and that they may teach their children.
DEUTERONOMY 4:9-10

PATIENCE

Be patient therefore, brethren, unto
the coming of the Lord. Behold, the
husbandman waiteth for the precious
fruit of the earth, and hath long
patience for it, until he receive the
early and latter rain. Be ye also patient;
stablish your hearts: for the coming of
the Lord draweth nigh.
JAMES 5:7–8

For what glory is it, if, when ye be
buffeted for your faults, ye shall take
it patiently? but if, when ye do well,
and suffer for it, ye take it patiently,
this is acceptable with God.
1 PETER 2:20

And let us not be weary in well
doing: for in due season we
shall reap, if we faint not.
GALATIANS 6:9

Let us hold fast the profession of our
faith without wavering; (for he is
faithful that promised).
HEBREWS 10:23

But he that shall endure unto the end,
the same shall be saved.
MATTHEW 24:13

That ye be not slothful, but followers
of them who through faith and
patience inherit the promises.
HEBREWS 6:12

For ye have need of patience, that,
after ye have done the will of God,
ye might receive the promise.
HEBREWS 10:36

> My brethren, count it all joy when
> ye fall into divers temptations;
> Knowing this, that the trying of
> your faith worketh patience.
> But let patience have her perfect
> work, that ye may be perfect and
> entire, wanting nothing.
> JAMES 1:2–4

And not only so, but we glory in
tribulations also: knowing that
tribulation worketh patience;
And patience, experience;
and experience, hope.
ROMANS 5:3–4

PEACE

Peace, peace to him that is far off,
and to him that is near, saith the
LORD; and I will heal him.
ISAIAH 57:19

And let the peace of God rule in your
hearts, to the which also ye are called
in one body; and be ye thankful.
COLOSSIANS 3:15

I will hear what God the LORD
will speak: for he will speak peace
unto his people, and to his saints.
PSALM 85:8

And the peace of God, which passeth
all understanding, shall keep your
hearts and minds through Christ Jesus.
PHILIPPIANS 4:7

And the work of righteousness shall be
peace; and the effect of righteousness
quietness and assurance for ever.
ISAIAH 32:17

Peace I leave with you, my peace I
give unto you: not as the world giveth,
give I unto you. Let not your heart be
troubled, neither let it be afraid.
JOHN 14:27

Mark the perfect man, and behold
the upright: for the end of that
man is peace.
PSALM 37:37

Thy faith hath saved
thee; go in peace.
LUKE 7:50

Now the Lord of peace himself give
you peace always by all means.
2 THESSALONIANS 3:16

POVERTY

For he shall deliver the needy when he crieth; the poor also, and him that hath no helper. He shall spare the poor and needy, and shall save the souls of the needy.
PSALM 72:12–13

Yet setteth he the poor on high from affliction, and maketh him families like a flock.
PSALM 107:41

For the LORD heareth the poor, and despiseth not his prisoners.
PSALM 69:33

Sing unto the LORD, praise ye the LORD: for he hath delivered the soul of the poor from the hand of evildoers.
JEREMIAH 20:13

He will regard the prayer of the destitute, and not despise their prayer.
PSALM 102:17

He raiseth up the poor out of the dust, and lifteth the needy out of the dunghill.
PSALM 113:7

I will abundantly bless her provision: I will satisfy her poor with bread.
PSALM 132:15

Thou, O God, hast prepared of thy goodness for the poor.
PSALM 68:10

PRAYER

Ask, and it shall be given you; seek,
and ye shall find; knock, and it shall
be opened unto you: For every one
that asketh receiveth; and he that
seeketh findeth; and to him that
knocketh it shall be opened.
MATTHEW 7:7–8

And all things, whatsoever ye shall ask
in prayer, believing, ye shall receive.
MATTHEW 21:22

He will be very gracious unto thee
at the voice of thy cry; when he
shall hear it, he will answer thee.
ISAIAH 30:19

And this is the confidence that
we have in him, that, if we ask
any thing according to his will,
he heareth us: And if we know
that he hear us, whatsoever we
ask, we know that we have the
petitions that we desired of him.
1 JOHN 5:14–15

And it shall come to pass, that before
they call, I will answer; and while
they are yet speaking, I will hear.
ISAIAH 65:24

Whatsoever ye shall ask the Father
in my name, he will give it you.
Hitherto have ye asked nothing in
my name: ask, and ye shall receive,
that your joy may be full.
JOHN 16:23–24

Confess your faults one to another,
and pray one for another, that ye may
be healed. The effectual fervent prayer
of a righteous man availeth much.
JAMES 5:16

And I say unto you, Ask, and it shall
be given you; seek, and ye shall find;
knock, and it shall be opened unto you.
LUKE 11:9

And whatsoever ye shall ask in my
name, that will I do, that the Father
may be glorified in the Son. If ye shall
ask any thing in my name, I will do it.
JOHN 14:13–14

If ye abide in me, and my words
abide in you, ye shall ask what ye
will, and it shall be done unto you.
JOHN 15:7

But thou, when thou prayest, enter
into thy closet, and when thou hast
shut thy door, pray to thy Father which
is in secret; and thy Father which seeth
in secret shall reward thee openly.
MATTHEW 6:6

He shall call upon me,
and I will answer him.
PSALM 91:15

The LORD is far from the wicked: but
he heareth the prayer of the righteous.
PROVERBS 15:29

O thou that hearest prayer,
unto thee shall all flesh come.
PSALM 65:2

The righteous cry, and the LORD
heareth, and delivereth them
out of all their troubles.
PSALM 34:17

If ye then, being evil, know how to
give good gifts unto your children,
how much more shall your Father
which is in heaven give good things
to them that ask him?
MATTHEW 7:11

Then shalt thou call, and the
LORD shall answer; thou shalt cry,
and he shall say, Here I am.
ISAIAH 58:9

Evening, and morning,
and at noon, will I pray, and cry
aloud: and he shall hear my voice.
PSALM 55:17

The LORD is nigh unto all them that
call upon him, to all that call upon
him in truth. He will fulfil the desire
of them that fear him: he also will hear
their cry, and will save them.
PSALM 145:18–19

Then shall ye call upon me,
and ye shall go and pray unto me,
and I will hearken unto you.
JEREMIAH 29:12

Be not ye therefore like unto them:
for your Father knoweth what things
ye have need of, before ye ask him.
MATTHEW 6:8

And I will bring the third part through
the fire, and will refine them as silver
is refined, and will try them as gold is
tried: they shall call on my name, and I
will hear them: I will say, It is my people:
and they shall say, The LORD is my God.
ZECHARIAH 13:9

And whatsoever we ask, we
receive of him, because we keep
his commandments, and do those
things that are pleasing in his sight.
I JOHN 3:22

PRIDE

Pride goeth before destruction,
and an haughty spirit before a fall.
PROVERBS 16:18

Woe unto them that are
wise in their own eyes, and
prudent in their own sight!
ISAIAH 5:21

Seest thou a man wise in his own
conceit? there is more hope of
a fool than of him.
PROVERBS 26:12

Look on every one that is proud,
and bring him low; and tread
down the wicked in their place.
JOB 40:12

An high look, and a proud heart,
and the plowing of the wicked, is sin.
PROVERBS 21:4

And he said unto them, Ye are they
which justify yourselves before men;
but God knoweth your hearts: for that
which is highly esteemed among men
is abomination in the sight of God.
LUKE 16:15

But he that glorieth, let him glory in
the Lord. For not he that commendeth
himself is approved, but whom the
Lord commendeth.
2 CORINTHIANS 10:17–18

The fear of the Lord is to hate evil:
pride, and arrogancy, and the evil way,
and the froward mouth, do I hate.
PROVERBS 8:13

Let another man praise thee,
and not thine own mouth;
a stranger, and not thine own lips.
PROVERBS 27:2

Thou hast rebuked the proud
that are cursed, which do err
from thy commandments.
PSALM 119:21

He that is of a proud heart stirreth
up strife: but he that putteth his
trust in the Lord shall be made fat.
He that trusteth in his own heart is
a fool: but whoso walketh wisely,
he shall be delivered.
PROVERBS 28:25–26

How can ye believe, which receive
honour one of another, and seek not the
honour that cometh from God only?
JOHN 5:44

And he sat down, and called the twelve,
and saith unto them, If any man desire
to be first, the same shall be last of all,
and servant of all.
MARK 9:35

PRISONERS

But thus saith the LORD, Even the captives of the mighty shall be taken away, and the prey of the terrible shall be delivered: for I will contend with him that contendeth with thee, and I will save thy children.
ISAIAH 49:25

If any of thine be driven out unto the outmost parts of heaven, from thence will the LORD thy God gather thee, and from thence will he fetch thee.
DEUTERONOMY 30:4

For the LORD heareth the poor, and despiseth not his prisoners.
PSALM 69:33

He brought them out of darkness and the shadow of death, and brake their bands in sunder.
PSALM 107:14

Which executeth judgment for the oppressed: which giveth food to the hungry. The LORD looseth the prisoners.
PSALM 146:7

God setteth the solitary in families: he bringeth out those which are bound with chains: but the rebellious dwell in a dry land.
PSALM 68:6

PROTECTION, GOD'S

The name of the Lord is a
strong tower: the righteous
runneth into it, and is safe.
Proverbs 18:10

> The angel of the Lord encampeth
> round about them that fear him,
> and delivereth them.
> Psalm 34:7

For the eyes of the Lord run to and
fro throughout the whole earth, to
shew himself strong in the behalf of
them whose heart is perfect toward
him. Herein thou hast done foolishly:
therefore from henceforth thou shalt
have wars.
2 Chronicles 16:9

> The Lord shall preserve thee from
> all evil: he shall preserve thy soul.
> The Lord shall preserve thy going
> out and thy coming in from this time
> forth, and even for evermore.
> Psalm 121:7–8

When thou liest down, thou shalt
not be afraid: yea, thou shalt lie down,
and thy sleep shall be sweet.
Proverbs 3:24

> And who is he that will harm you, if ye
> be followers of that which is good?
> 1 Peter 3:13

The beloved of the LORD shall dwell
in safety by him; and the Lord shall
cover him all the day long, and he
shall dwell between his shoulders.
DEUTERONOMY 33:12

He shall not be afraid of evil tidings:
his heart is fixed, trusting in the LORD.
PSALM 112:7

Because thou hast made the LORD,
which is my refuge, even the most
High, thy habitation; There shall no
evil befall thee, neither shall any
plague come nigh thy dwelling.
PSALM 91:9–10

And they shall no more be a prey to the
heathen, neither shall the beast of the
land devour them; but they shall dwell
safely, and none shall make them afraid.
EZEKIEL 34:28

But whoso hearkeneth unto me
shall dwell safely, and shall be
quiet from fear of evil.
PROVERBS 1:33

I will both lay me down in peace,
and sleep: for thou, LORD, only
makest me dwell in safety.
PSALM 4:8

The LORD is my light and my
salvation; whom shall I fear?
the LORD is the strength of my life;
of whom shall I be afraid?
PSALM 27:1

REPENTANCE

The time is fulfilled, and the
kingdom of God is at hand:
repent ye, and believe the gospel.
MARK 1:15

> And they went out, and preached
> that men should repent.
> MARK 6:12

The LORD is nigh unto them that
are of a broken heart; and saveth
such as be of a contrite spirit.
PSALM 34:18

> He healeth the broken in heart,
> and bindeth up their wounds.
> PSALM 147:3

Repent ye therefore, and be converted,
that your sins may be blotted out,
when the times of refreshing shall
come from the presence of the Lord.
ACTS 3:19

> For I am not come to call the
> righteous, but sinners to repentance.
> MATTHEW 9:13

But if the wicked will turn from
all his sins that he hath committed,
and keep all my statutes, and do that
which is lawful and right, he shall
surely live, he shall not die. All his
transgressions that he hath committed,
they shall not be mentioned unto him:
in his righteousness that he hath
done he shall live.
EZEKIEL 18:21–22

RIGHTEOUSNESS

For the LORD God is a sun and shield:
the LORD will give grace and glory:
no good thing will he withhold from
them that walk uprightly.
PSALM 84:11

The young lions do lack, and suffer
hunger: but they that seek the LORD
shall not want any good thing.
PSALM 34:10

The fear of the wicked, it shall come
upon him: but the desire of the
righteous shall be granted.
PROVERBS 10:24

Evil pursueth sinners: but to the
righteous good shall be repayed.
PROVERBS 13:21

A good man obtaineth favour of the
LORD: but a man of wicked devices
will he condemn.
PROVERBS 12:2

But seek ye first the kingdom of God,
and his righteousness; and all these
things shall be added unto you.
MATTHEW 6:33

He that trusteth in his riches shall
fall; but the righteous shall flourish
as a branch.
PROVERBS 11:28

So that a man shall say, Verily there
is a reward for the righteous.

PSALM 58:11

For thou, LORD, wilt bless the
righteous; with favour wilt thou
compass him as with a shield.

PSALM 5:12

Salvation belongeth unto the LORD:
thy blessing is upon thy people.

PSALM 3:8

Whether Paul, or Apollos, or Cephas,
or the world, or life, or death,
or things present, or things to come;
all are yours; And ye are Christ's;
and Christ is God's.

1 CORINTHIANS 3:22–23

He that spared not his own Son,
but delivered him up for us all,
how shall he not with him also
freely give us all things?

ROMANS 8:32

Say ye to the righteous, that it shall
be well with him: for they shall
eat the fruit of their doings.

ISAIAH 3:10

Surely goodness and mercy shall follow
me all the days of my life: and I will
dwell in the house of the LORD for ever.

PSALM 23:6

SALVATION

Therefore if any man be in Christ, he is a new creature: old things are passed away; behold, all things are become new.
2 CORINTHIANS 5:17

For he hath made him to be sin for us, who knew no sin; that we might be made the righteousness of God in him.
2 CORINTHIANS 5:21

And you hath he quickened, who were dead in trespasses and sins.
EPHESIANS 2:1

For this is good and acceptable in the sight of God our Saviour; Who will have all men to be saved, and to come unto the knowledge of the truth.
1 TIMOTHY 2:3-4

My little children, these things write I unto you, that ye sin not. And if any man sin, we have an advocate with the Father, Jesus Christ the righteous: And he is the propitiation for our sins: and not for ours only, but also for the sins of the whole world.
1 JOHN 2:1-2

And you, being dead in your sins and the uncircumcision of your flesh, hath he quickened together with him, having forgiven you all trespasses.
COLOSSIANS 2:13

This is a faithful saying and worthy of
all acceptation. For therefore we both
labour and suffer reproach, because
we trust in the living God, who is the
Saviour of all men, specially of those
that believe.

1 TIMOTHY 4:9–10

> But not as the offence, so also is the
> free gift. For if through the offence of
> one many be dead, much more the
> grace of God, and the gift by grace,
> which is by one man, Jesus Christ,
> hath abounded unto many.
>
> ROMANS 5:15

But after that the kindness and love of
God our Saviour toward man appeared,
Not by works of righteousness which
we have done, but according to his
mercy he saved us, by the washing
of regeneration, and renewing of the
Holy Ghost; Which he shed on us
abundantly through Jesus Christ
our Saviour.

TITUS 3:4–6

> But as many as received him, to them
> gave he power to become the sons of
> God, even to them that believe on his
> name: Which were born, not of blood,
> nor of the will of the flesh, nor of the
> will of man, but of God.
>
> JOHN 1:12–13

SEEKING GOD

The LORD is with you, while ye
be with him; and if ye seek him,
he will be found of you; but if ye
forsake him, he will forsake you.
2 CHRONICLES 15:2

Sow to yourselves in righteousness,
reap in mercy; break up your
fallow ground: for it is time to seek
the LORD, till he come and rain
righteousness upon you.
HOSEA 10:12

But without faith it is impossible
to please him: for he that cometh
to God must believe that he is,
and that he is a rewarder of them
that diligently seek him.
HEBREWS 11:6

That they should seek the Lord,
if haply they might feel after him,
and find him, though he be not
far from every one of us.
ACTS 17:27

The LORD is good unto them that wait
for him, to the soul that seeketh him.
LAMENTATIONS 3:25

For thus saith the LORD unto the house
of Israel, Seek ye me, and ye shall live.
AMOS 5:4

The hand of our God is upon
all them for good that seek him;
but his power and his wrath is
against all them that forsake him.
Ezra 8:22

> But if from thence thou shalt seek
> the Lord thy God, thou shalt find
> him, if you seek him with all thy
> heart and with all thy soul.
> Deuteronomy 4:29

And thou, Solomon my son, know
thou the God of thy father, and serve
him with a perfect heart and with a
willing mind: for the Lord searcheth
all hearts, and understandeth all the
imaginations of the thoughts: if thou
seek him, he will be found of thee; but
if thou forsake him, he will cast thee
off for ever.
1 Chronicles 28:9

> And they that know thy name will put
> their trust in thee: for thou, Lord, hast
> not forsaken them that seek thee.
> Psalm 9:10

SELF-DENIAL

Then said Jesus unto his disciples,
If any man will come after me, let him
deny himself, and take up his cross,
and follow me. For whosoever will save
his life shall lose it: and whosoever will
lose his life for my sake shall find it.
For what is a man profited, if he shall
gain the whole world, and lose his
own soul? or what shall a man give
in exchange for his soul?
MATTHEW 16:24–26

Therefore, brethren, we are debtors,
not to the flesh, to live after the flesh.
For if ye live after the flesh, ye shall die:
but if ye through the Spirit do mortify
the deeds of the body, ye shall live.
ROMANS 8:12-13

For the grace of God that bringeth
salvation hath appeared to all men,
Teaching us that, denying ungodliness
and worldly lusts, we should live
soberly, righteously, and godly,
in this present world.
TITUS 2:11–12

And they that are Christ's
have crucified the flesh with
the affections and lusts.
GALATIANS 5:24

But I say unto you, That ye resist not evil: but whosoever shall smite thee on thy right cheek, turn to him the other also. And if any man will sue thee at the law, and take away thy coat, let him have thy cloak also. And whosoever shall compel thee to go a mile, go with him twain.

MATTHEW 5:39–41

And he said unto them, Verily I say unto you, There is no man that hath left house, or parents, or brethren, or wife, or children, for the kingdom of God's sake, Who shall not receive manifold more in this present time, and in the world to come life everlasting.

LUKE 18:29-30

SELF-RIGHTEOUSNESS

There is a generation that are pure
in their own eyes, and yet is not
washed from their filthiness. There
is a generation, O how lofty are their
eyes! and their eyelids are lifted up.
PROVERBS 30:12–13

> The way of a fool is right in his
> own eyes: but he that hearkeneth
> unto counsel is wise.
> PROVERBS 12:15

Woe unto them that are wise
in their own eyes, and prudent
in their own sight!
ISAIAH 5:21

> Yet thou sayest, Because I am innocent,
> surely his anger shall turn from me.
> Behold, I will plead with thee, because
> thou sayest, I have not sinned.
> JEREMIAH 2:35

Seest thou a man wise in his
own conceit? there is more hope
of a fool than of him.
PROVERBS 26:12

> But he that glorieth, let him glory
> in the Lord. For not he that
> commendeth himself is approved,
> but whom the Lord commendeth.
> 2 CORINTHIANS 10:17–18

He that is of a proud heart stirreth up
strife: but he that putteth his trust in
the Lord shall be made fat. He that
trusteth in his own heart is a fool:
but whoso walketh wisely,
he shall be delivered.
Proverbs 28:25–26

> For if a man think himself to be
> something, when he is nothing,
> he deceiveth himself.
> Galatians 6:3

Let another man praise thee,
and not thine own mouth;
a stranger, and not thine own lips.
Proverbs 27:2

> Jesus said unto them, If ye were blind,
> ye should have no sin: but now ye say,
> We see; therefore your sin remaineth.
> John 9:41

But we are all as an unclean thing,
and all our righteousnesses are as
filthy rags; and we all do fade as a leaf;
and our iniquities, like the wind,
have taken us away.
Isaiah 64:6

> And he said unto them, Ye are they
> which justify yourselves before men;
> but God knoweth your hearts: for that
> which is highly esteemed among men
> is abomination in the sight of God.
> Luke 16:15

SEXUAL SINS

Now the body is not for fornication,
but for the Lord; and the Lord
for the body.
1 CORINTHIANS 6:13

There hath no temptation taken
you but such as is common to man:
but God is faithful, who will not suffer
you to be tempted above that ye are
able; but will with the temptation also
make a way to escape, that ye may
be able to bear it.
1 CORINTHIANS 10:13

Now concerning the things whereof
ye wrote unto me: It is good for
a man not to touch a woman.
1 CORINTHIANS 7:1

I say therefore to the unmarried
and widows, it is good for them if
they abide even as I. But if they
cannot contain, let them marry:
for it is better to marry than to burn.
1 CORINTHIANS 7:8–9

Nevertheless he that standeth stedfast
in his heart, having no necessity,
but hath power over his own will,
and hath so decreed in his heart
that he will keep his virgin, doeth well.
1 CORINTHIANS 7:37

Marriage is honourable in all, and the
bed undefiled: but whoremongers
and adulterers God will judge.
HEBREWS 13:4

These are they which were not defiled
with women; for they are virgins.
These are they which follow the Lamb
whithersoever he goeth. These were
redeemed from among men, being the
firstfruits unto God and to the Lamb.
REVELATION 14:4

For this is the will of God, even
your sanctification, that ye should
abstain from fornication.
1 THESSALONIANS 4:3

Know ye not that your bodies are the
members of Christ? shall I then take
the members of Christ, and make them
the members of an harlot? God forbid.
1 CORINTHIANS 6:15

Who can find a virtuous woman?
for her price is far above rubies.
PROVERBS 31:10

The Lord knoweth how to deliver
the godly out of temptations, and
to reserve the unjust unto the day of
judgment to be punished.
2 PETER 2:9

Blessed is the man that endureth
temptation: for when he is tried,
he shall receive the crown of life,
which the Lord hath promised
to them that love him.

JAMES 1:12

For in that he himself hath suffered
being tempted, he is able to succour
them that are tempted.
HEBREWS 2:18

For we have not an high priest
which cannot be touched with the
feeling of our infirmities; but was in
all points tempted like as we are, yet
without sin. Let us therefore come
boldly unto the throne of grace, that
we may obtain mercy, and find grace
to help in time of need.

HEBREWS 4:15–16

SHAME

For the scripture saith, Whosoever believeth on him shall not be ashamed.
ROMANS 10:11

> Then shall I not be ashamed, when I have respect unto all thy commandments.
> PSALM 119:6

And hope maketh not ashamed; because the love of God is shed abroad in our hearts by the Holy Ghost which is given unto us.
ROMANS 5:5

> For the which cause I also suffer these things: nevertheless I am not ashamed: for I know whom I have believed, and am persuaded that he is able to keep that which I have committed unto him against that day.
> 2 TIMOTHY 1:12

As it is written, Behold, I lay in Sion a stumblingstone and rock of offence: and whosoever believeth on him shall not be ashamed.
ROMANS 9:33

> Study to shew thyself approved unto God, a workman that needeth not to be ashamed, rightly dividing the word of truth.
> 2 TIMOTHY 2:15

Let my heart be sound in thy statutes;
that I be not ashamed.
PSALM 119:80

Yet if any man suffer as a Christian,
let him not be ashamed; but let him
glorify God on this behalf.
1 PETER 4:16

SICKNESS

Is any sick among you? let him call for the elders of the church; and let them pray over him, anointing him with oil in the name of the Lord: And the prayer of faith shall save the sick, and the Lord shall raise him up; and if he have committed sins, they shall be forgiven him. Confess your faults one to another, and pray one for another, that ye may be healed. The effectual fervent prayer of a righteous man availeth much.
JAMES 5:14–16

And when he was come into the house, the blind men came to him: and Jesus saith unto them, Believe ye that I am able to do this? They said unto him, Yea, Lord. Then touched he their eyes, saying, According to your faith be it unto you. And their eyes were opened.
MATTHEW 9:28-30

Heal me, O LORD, and I shall be healed; save me, and I shall be saved: for thou art my praise.
JEREMIAH 17:14

But that ye may know that the Son of man hath power on earth to forgive sins, (then saith he to the sick of the palsy,) Arise, take up thy bed, and go unto thine house. And he arose, and departed to his house.
MATTHEW 9:6-7

For I will restore health unto thee,
and I will heal thee of thy wounds,
saith the LORD.
JEREMIAH 30:17

And ye shall serve the LORD your
God, and he shall bless thy bread,
and thy water; and I will take sickness
away from the midst of thee.
EXODUS 23:25

Who his own self bare our sins in
his own body on the tree, that we,
being dead to sins, should live unto
righteousness: by whose stripes ye
were healed.
1 PETER 2:24

But he was wounded for our
transgressions, he was bruised for
our iniquities: the chastisement of
our peace was upon him; and with
his stripes we are healed.
ISAIAH 53:5

SIN, FREEDOM FROM

Then will I sprinkle clean water upon you, and ye shall be clean: from all your filthiness, and from all your idols, will I cleanse you. A new heart also will I give you, and a new spirit will I put within you: and I will take away the stony heart out of your flesh, and I will give you an heart of flesh.
EZEKIEL 36:25–26

To him give all the prophets witness, that through his name whosoever believeth in him shall receive remission of sins.
ACTS 10:43

Knowing this, that our old man is crucified with him, that the body of sin might be destroyed, that henceforth we should not serve sin. For he that is dead is freed from sin.
ROMANS 6:6–7

Therefore if any man be in Christ, he is a new creature: old things are passed away; behold, all things are become new.
2 CORINTHIANS 5:17

What shall we say then? Shall we continue in sin, that grace may abound? God forbid. How shall we, that are dead to sin, live any longer therein?
ROMANS 6:1–2

For sin shall not have dominion over you: for ye are not under the law, but under grace.
ROMANS 6:14

Likewise reckon ye also yourselves to be dead indeed unto sin, but alive unto God through Jesus Christ our Lord.
ROMANS 6:11

SIN, REDEMPTION FROM

And she shall bring forth a son, and
thou shalt call his name Jesus: for he
shall save his people from their sins.
MATTHEW 1:21

> Be it known unto you therefore,
> men and brethren, that through
> this man is preached unto you
> the forgiveness of sins.
> ACTS 13:38

Who gave himself for our sins,
that he might deliver us from this
present evil world, according to
the will of God and our Father.
GALATIANS 1:4

> And if any man sin, we have an
> advocate with the Father, Jesus
> Christ the righteous: And he is the
> propitiation for our sins: and not
> for ours only, but also for the sins
> of the whole world.
> 1 JOHN 2:1–2

Who his own self bare our sins in
his own body on the tree, that we,
being dead to sins, should live unto
righteousness: by whose stripes ye
were healed.
1 PETER 2:24

This is a faithful saying, and worthy of all acceptation, that Christ Jesus came into the world to save sinners; of whom I am chief.
1 TIMOTHY 1:15

For by one offering he hath perfected for ever them that are sanctified.
HEBREWS 10:14

The next day John seeth Jesus coming unto him, and saith, Behold the Lamb of God, which taketh away the sin of the world.
JOHN 1:29

But he was wounded for our transgressions, he was bruised for our iniquities: the chastisement of our peace was upon him; and with his stripes we are healed. All we like sheep have gone astray; we have turned every one to his own way; and the LORD hath laid on him in the iniquity of us all.
ISAIAH 53:5–6

In whom we have redemption through his blood, the forgiveness of sins, according to the riches of his grace.
EPHESIANS 1:7

And ye know that he was manifested to take away our sins; and in him is no sin.
1 JOHN 3:5

So Christ was once offered to bear the sins of many; and unto them that look for him shall he appear the second time without sin unto salvation.

HEBREWS 9:28

For this is my blood of the new testament, which is shed for many for the remission of sins.
MATTHEW 26:28

SLANDER AND REPROACH

Blessed are ye, when men shall revile
you, and persecute you, and shall say
all manner of evil against you falsely,
for my sake. Rejoice, and be exceeding
glad: for great is your reward in heaven:
for so persecuted they the prophets
which were before you.
MATTHEW 5:11–12

> If ye be reproached for the name of
> Christ, happy are ye; for the spirit of
> glory and of God resteth upon you:
> on their part he is evil spoken of,
> but on your part he is glorified.
> 1 PETER 4:14

Hearken unto me, ye that know
righteousness, the people in whose
heart is my law; fear ye not the
reproach of men, neither be ye
afraid of their revilings.
ISAIAH 51:7

> Thou shalt hide them in the secret of
> thy presence from the pride of man:
> thou shalt keep them secretly in a
> pavilion from the strife of tongues.
> PSALM 31:20

And he shall bring forth thy
righteousness as the light, and
thy judgment as the noonday.
PSALM 37:6

And ye shall be hated of all men for
my name's sake: but he that endureth
to the end shall be saved.

MATTHEW 10:22

SUCCESS

In the house of the righteous is
much treasure: but in the revenues
of the wicked is trouble.
PROVERBS 15:6

> By humility and the fear of the LORD
> are riches, and honour, and life.
> PROVERBS 22:4

And the LORD thy God will make thee
plenteous in every work of thine hand,
in the fruit of thy body, and in the
fruit of thy cattle, and in the fruit of
thy land, for good: for the Lord will
again rejoice over thee for good, as he
rejoiced over thy fathers.
DEUTERONOMY 30:9

> And also that every man should eat
> and drink, and enjoy the good of
> all his labour, it is the gift of God.
> ECCLESIASTES 3:13

Every man also to whom God hath
given riches and wealth, and hath
given him power to eat thereof, and to
take his portion, and to rejoice in his
labour; this is the gift of God.
ECCLESIASTES 5:19

> And I will send grass in thy
> fields for thy cattle, that thou
> mayest eat and be full.
> DEUTERONOMY 11:15

And he shall be like a tree planted by
the rivers of water, that bringeth forth
his fruit in his season; his leaf also shall
not wither; and whatsoever he doeth
shall prosper.
PSALM 1:3

Then shall he give the rain of thy
seed, that thou shalt sow the ground
withal; and bread of the increase of
the earth, and it shall be fat and
plenteous: in that day shall thy
cattle feed in large pastures.
ISAIAH 30:23

Riches and honour are with me;
yea, durable riches and righteousness.
My fruit is better than gold, yea,
than fine gold; and my revenue
than choice silver.
PROVERBS 8:18–19

Wealth and riches shall be in
his house: and his righteousness
endureth for ever.
PSALM 112:3

According as his divine power hath
given unto us all things that pertain
unto life and godliness, through the
knowledge of him that hath called us
to glory and virtue.
2 PETER 1:3

But grow in grace, and in the
knowledge of our Lord and Saviour
Jesus Christ. To him be glory both
now and for ever. Amen.
2 PETER 3:18

For thou shalt eat the labour of thine
hands: happy shalt thou be, and it
shall be well with thee.
PSALM 128:2

TRUST

God is our refuge and strength, a very present help in trouble. Therefore will not we fear, though the earth be removed, and though the mountains be carried into the midst of the sea.
PSALM 46:1–2

> For the LORD God is a sun and shield: the LORD will give grace and glory: no good thing will he withhold from them that walk uprightly. O LORD of hosts, blessed is the man that trusteth in thee.
> PSALM 84:11–12

Trust in the LORD, and do good; so shalt thou dwell in the land, and verily thou shalt be fed. Delight thyself also in the LORD: and he shall give thee the desires of thine heart. Commit thy way unto the LORD; trust also in him; and he shall bring it to pass.
PSALM 37:3–5

> Trust in the LORD with all thine heart; and lean not unto thine own understanding. In all thy ways acknowledge him, and he shall direct thy paths.
> PROVERBS 3:5–6

Fear not, little flock; for it is your Father's good pleasure to give you the kingdom.
LUKE 12:32

Casting all your care upon him;
for he careth for you.
1 PETER 5:7

They that trust in the LORD shall be
as mount Zion, which cannot be
removed, but abideth for ever.
PSALM 125:1

Therefore take no thought, saying,
What shall we eat? or, What shall we
drink? or, Wherewithal shall we be
clothed? (For after all these things do
the Gentiles seek:) for your heavenly
Father knoweth that ye have need
of all these things.
MATTHEW 6:31–32

Blessed is that man that
maketh the LORD his trust.
PSALM 40:4

WISDOM

If any of you lack wisdom, let him
ask of God, that giveth to all men
liberally, and upbraideth not; and it
shall be given him.
JAMES 1:5

> And he will teach us of his ways,
> and we will walk in his paths.
> ISAIAH 2:3

I will instruct thee and teach thee in
the way which thou shalt go: I will
guide thee with mine eye.
PSALM 32:8

> For God giveth to a man that
> is good in his sight wisdom,
> and knowledge, and joy.
> ECCLESIASTES 2:26

I will bless the LORD, who hath given
me counsel: my reins also instruct me
in the night seasons.
PSALM 16:7

> Then shalt thou understand the fear
> of the LORD, and find the knowledge of
> God. For the LORD giveth wisdom: out
> of his mouth cometh knowledge and
> understanding. He layeth up sound
> wisdom for the righteous: he is a
> buckler to them that walk uprightly.
> PROVERBS 2:5-7

Evil men understand not judgment:
but they that seek the LORD
understand all things.
PROVERBS 28:5

And we know that the Son of God
is come, and hath given us an
understanding, that we may know him
that is true, and we are in him that is
true, even in his Son Jesus Christ. This
is the true God, and eternal life.
1 JOHN 5:20

For God, who commanded the light
to shine out of darkness, hath shined
in our hearts, to give the light of the
knowledge of the glory of God in
the face of Jesus Christ.
2 CORINTHIANS 4:6

Behold, thou desirest truth in the
inward parts: and in the hidden part
thou shalt make me to know wisdom.
PSALM 51:6

WORD OF GOD

For I am not ashamed of the gospel of
Christ: for it is the power of God unto
salvation to every one that believeth.
ROMANS 1:16

> Blessed is he that readeth, and they
> that hear the words of this prophecy,
> and keep those things which are
> written therein: for the time is at hand.
> REVELATION 1:3

We have also a more sure word of
prophecy; whereunto ye do well
that ye take heed, as unto a light
that shineth in a dark place, until the
day dawn, and the day star arise in
your hearts.
2 PETER 1:19

> For the word of God is quick, and
> powerful, and sharper than any
> twoedged sword, piercing even to
> the dividing asunder of soul and
> spirit, and of the joints and marrow,
> and is a discerner of the thoughts
> and intents of the heart.
> HEBREWS 4:12

Search the scriptures; for in them
ye think ye have eternal life: and
they are they which testify of me.
JOHN 5:39

For the commandment is a lamp;
and the law is light; and reproofs of
instruction are the way of life.

PROVERBS 6:23

The entrance of thy words giveth
light; it giveth understanding unto
the simple.

PSALM 119:130

The holy scriptures, which are able
to make thee wise unto salvation
through faith which is in Christ Jesus.
All scripture is given by inspiration of
God, and is profitable for doctrine,
for reproof, for correction,
for instruction in righteousness.

2 TIMOTHY 3:15–16

So then faith cometh by hearing,
and hearing by the word of God.

ROMANS 10:17

As newborn babes, desire
the sincere milk of the word,
that ye may grow thereby.

1 PETER 2:2

Therefore shall ye lay up these my
words in your heart and in your soul,
and bind them for a sign upon your
hand, that they may be as frontlets
between your eyes.

DEUTERONOMY 11:18

This book of the law shall not depart
out of thy mouth; but thou shalt
meditate therein day and night,
that thou mayest observe to do
according to all that is written therein:
for then thou shalt make thy way
prosperous, and then thou shalt
have good success.

JOSHUA 1:8

And now, brethren, I commend you
to God, and to the word of his grace,
which is able to build you up, and to
give you an inheritance among all
them which are sanctified.
ACTS 20:32

Thy word is a lamp unto my feet,
and a light unto my path.

PSALM 119:105

Being born again, not of corruptible
seed, but of incorruptible, by the word
of God, which liveth and abideth
for ever.
1 PETER 1:23

WORK

And God blessed the seventh day, and sanctified it: because that in it he had rested from all his work which God created and made.
GENESIS 2:3

The LORD shall open unto thee his good treasure, the heaven to give the rain unto thy land in his season, and to bless all the work of thine hand: and thou shalt lend unto many nations, and thou shalt not borrow.
DEUTERONOMY 28:12

Be ye strong therefore, and let not your hands be weak: for your work shall be rewarded.
2 CHRONICLES 15:7

And in every work that he began in the service of the house of God, and in the law, and in the commandments, to seek his God, he did it with all his heart, and prospered.
2 CHRONICLES 31:21

Even a child is known by his doings, whether his work be pure, and whether it be right.
PROVERBS 20:11

In all labour there is profit: but the talk of the lips tendeth only to penury.
PROVERBS 14:23

Then said they unto him, What shall we do, that we might work the works of God? Jesus answered and said unto them, This is the work of God, that ye believe on him whom he hath sent.

JOHN 6:28–29

Jesus saith unto them, My meat is to do the will of him that sent me, and to finish his work.

JOHN 4:34

I have glorified thee on the earth: I have finished the work which thou gavest me to do. And now, O Father, glorify thou me with thine own self with the glory which I had with thee before the world was.

JOHN 17:4–5

Therefore, my beloved brethren, be ye stedfast, unmoveable, always abounding in the work of the Lord, forasmuch as ye know that your labour is not in vain in the Lord.

1 CORINTHIANS 15:58

That ye might walk worthy of the Lord unto all pleasing, being fruitful in every good work, and increasing in the knowledge of God.

COLOSSIANS 1:10

Come unto me, all ye that labour and are heavy laden, and I will give you rest.

MATTHEW 11:28

For we hear that there are some which walk among you disorderly, working not at all, but are busybodies. Now them that are such we command and exhort by our Lord Jesus Christ, that with quietness they work, and eat their own bread.

2 THESSALONIANS 3:11–12

> Except the LORD build the house,
> they labour in vain that build it:
> except the LORD keep the city,
> the watchman waketh but in vain.
>
> PSALM 127:1

Let him that stole steal no more: but rather let him labour, working with his hands the thing which is good, that he may have to give to him that needeth.

EPHESIANS 4:28

WORRY

Be careful for nothing; but in every
thing by prayer and supplication
with thanksgiving let your requests
be made known unto God. And
the peace of God, which passeth all
understanding, shall keep your hearts
and minds through Christ Jesus.
PHILIPPIANS 4:6–7

God is our refuge and strength, a very
present help in trouble. Therefore
will not we fear, though the earth be
removed, and though the mountains
be carried into the midst of the sea;
Though the waters thereof roar and be
troubled, though the mountains shake
with the swelling thereof.
PSALM 46:1–3

For he shall be as a tree planted by
the waters, and that spreadeth out her
roots by the river, and shall not see
when heat cometh, but her leaf shall
be green; and shall not be careful in
the year of drought, neither shall cease
from yielding fruit.
JEREMIAH 17:8

He shall call upon me, and I will answer
him: I will be with him in trouble; I will
deliver him, and honour him.
PSALM 91:15

But my God shall supply all your need according to his riches in glory by Christ Jesus.
PHILIPPIANS 4:19

And Jesus answered and said unto her, Martha, Martha, thou art careful and troubled about many things: But one thing is needful: and Mary hath chosen that good part, which shall not be taken away from her.
LUKE 10:41–42

The LORD also will be a refuge for the oppressed, a refuge in times of trouble. And they that know thy name will put their trust in thee: for thou, LORD, hast not forsaken them that seek thee.
PSALM 9:9–10

Thou art my hiding place; thou shalt preserve me from trouble; thou shalt compass me about with songs of deliverance.
PSALM 32:7

We are troubled on every side, yet not distressed; we are perplexed, but not in despair; Persecuted, but not forsaken; cast down, but not destroyed.
2 CORINTHIANS 4:8–9

And the work of righteousness shall be peace; and the effect of righteousness quietness and assurance for ever.
ISAIAH 32:17

And we know that all things work together for good to them that love God, to them who are the called according to his purpose.

ROMANS 8:28

WORSHIP

All the earth shall worship thee,
and shall sing unto thee; they
shall sing to thy name.
PSALM 66:4

O come, let us worship and bow
down: let us kneel before the
LORD our maker. For he is our God;
and we are the people of his pasture,
and the sheep of his hand.
PSALM 95:6–7

Exalt the LORD our God,
and worship at his holy hill;
for the LORD our God is holy.
PSALM 99:9

Now when Jesus was born in
Bethlehem of Judaea in the days of
Herod the king, behold, there came
wise men from the east to Jerusalem,
Saying, Where is he that is born King of
the Jews? for we have seen his star in
the east, and are come to worship him.
MATTHEW 2:1–2

Who shall not fear thee, O Lord, and
glorify thy name? for thou only art
holy: for all nations shall come and
worship before thee; for thy judgments
are made manifest.
REVELATION 15:4

The four and twenty elders fall down
before him that sat on the throne,
and worship him that liveth for ever and
ever, and cast their crowns before the
throne, saying, Thou art worthy, O Lord,
to receive glory and honour and power:
for thou hast created all things, and for
thy pleasure they are and were created.

REVELATION 4:10–11

All nations whom thou hast made
shall come and worship before thee,
O Lord; and shall glorify thy name.
PSALM 86:9

God is a Spirit: and they that
worship him must worship
him in spirit and in truth.

JOHN 4:24

And I fell at his feet to worship him.
And he said unto me, See thou do it
not: I am thy fellowservant, and of thy
brethren that have the testimony of
Jesus: worship God: for the testimony
of Jesus is the spirit of prophecy.
REVELATION 19:10

I will praise the LORD according to his
righteousness: and will sing praise to
the name of the LORD most high.

PSALM 7:17

And the devil said unto him, All this power will I give thee, and the glory of them: for that is delivered unto me; and to whomsoever I will I give it. If thou therefore wilt worship me, all shall be thine. And Jesus answered and said unto him, Get thee behind me, Satan: for it is written, Thou shalt worship the Lord thy God, and him only shalt thou serve.
LUKE 4:6–8

And, behold, there came a leper and worshipped him, saying, Lord, if thou wilt, thou canst make me clean. And Jesus put forth his hand, and touched him, saying, I will; be thou clean. And immediately his leprosy was cleansed.
MATTHEW 8:2-3

And the four and twenty elders, which sat before God on their seats, fell upon their faces, and worshipped God, Saying, We give thee thanks, O LORD God Almighty, which art, and wast, and art to come; because thou hast taken to thee thy great power, and hast reigned.
REVELATION 11:16–17